# NOTTINGHAM:
## TRAMWAY TO EXPRESS TRANSIT

### METRO & LIGHT RAIL SYSTEMS IN FOCUS

## ALAN YEARSLEY & ROBERT PRITCHARD

PLATFORM
5

© 2022 Platform 5 Publishing Ltd. All rights reserved. No part of this publication may be reproduced or transmitted in any form or by any means electronic, mechanical, photocopying, recording or otherwise, without prior permission of the publisher.

Published by Platform 5 Publishing Ltd, 52 Broadfield Road, Sheffield, S8 0XJ. England.

Printed in England by The Amadeus Press, Cleckheaton, West Yorkshire

ISBN: 978 1 909431 96 6

**Front cover (top left):** Nottingham's original tramway closed back in 1936. In this undated photo double-deck car 72 is seen in Bulwell Market Place after arrival with a route 3 service from Trent Bridge. *National Tramway Museum collection*

**Front cover (top right):** Bombardier Incentro tram 212 has just crossed Fairham Brook as it approaches the Southchurch Drive North stop on the Clifton South line on 17 July 2016. *Robert Pritchard*

**Front cover (main photo):** Alstom Citadis tram 228 leaves the busy Old Market Square stop in the bustling heart of Nottingham city centre with a Hucknall–Toton Lane service on 30 June 2018. *Robert Pritchard*

**Back cover:** On a snowy 30 December 2014, Incentro 205 arrives at the Phoenix Park terminus with a service from Nottingham Station. *Robert Pritchard*

# CONTENTS

# INTRODUCTION

It is now 18 years since the opening of the Nottingham Express Transit (NET) light rail system. Since then NET has established itself as an invaluable part of the East Midlands city's public transport network, even if a number of other extensions have been proposed but have not so far materialised. Nonetheless, the system has grown from just one line from the city centre to Hucknall in the north plus a short branch to Phoenix Park, to a more sizeable but still relatively compact network also serving the south and south-west Nottingham suburbs.

This book provides an ultimate present-day guide to the NET system, its background, history, operations and vehicle fleets. Although the main purpose of this book is to cover the present-day network, we have also included historical material on Nottingham's first generation tramway and trolleybus system.

This is the third in our series of books covering the UK tram and light rail systems following those on Sheffield Supertram and Manchester Metrolink: it is planned to produce a similar publication for each network over the coming years. As they are published, these will be advertised in our monthly magazines **Today's Railways UK** and **Today's Railways Europe**, on the Platform 5 Publishing website, and in our mail order catalogues and circulars.

We hope you will find this book an interesting and useful source of information. It draws on extensive research trips to Nottingham by both co-authors, original material from the launch of NET and also from a number of earlier Platform 5 publications, including our own UK Metro & Light Rail Systems handbook, various editions of the Light Rail Review series published in the late 1980s and 1990s, and back copies of **entrain** and **Today's Railways UK** magazines from the 2000s onwards.

We have made every effort to ensure that all information is correct at the time of going to press but cannot be held responsible for any errors or omissions. Nonetheless, any corrections or suggestions for improvements for future editions would be most gratefully received. Any comments on this publication can be addressed to the authors by e-mail at **alan.yearsley@platform5.com / robert.pritchard@platform5.com** or by post to the Platform 5 address on the title page.

## ACKNOWLEDGEMENTS

Most of the photographs used in this book have been drawn from many dozens of personal trips by the authors to Nottingham to both ride on and photograph the tramway since it opened in 2004, and we were pleased to have been able to illustrate all 37 of the existing fleet of Nottingham trams at least once within the pages of this book! We are also indebted to Mike Haddon for the use of his excellent construction photos of both NET Phase 1 and Phase 2. In addition, we would also like to extend our thanks to the Light Rail Transit Association (LRTA) and the staff of Nottingham Express Transit – especially tram driver Daniel Patterson – who organised an excellent behind-the-scenes visit to the depot and control centre at Wilkinson Street in 2019. We also extend our thanks to the National Tramway Museum and the British Trolleybus Society for access to their archive photographic collections and to Geoffrey Skelsey for his proof checking.

If readers have any photos that they would like to be considered for our forthcoming light rail system guidebooks (particularly any illustrating the early years of operation) please do get in touch using the email **pictures@platform5.com**.

## UPDATES

Any major developments with Nottingham Express Transit, and the country's other light rail and tram systems, can be found in the magazine **Today's Railways UK**. This is available at all good newsagents or on post-free subscription. Please see the inside covers of this book or the Platform 5 website for further details.

**Alan Yearsley & Robert Pritchard. February 2022.**

**Below:** Carrying the latest and third different livery applied to the original Bombardier Incentro trams, 213 "Mary Potter" arrives at Bulwell with a Sunday afternoon service from Hucknall to Toton Lane on 10 October 2021. *Robert Pritchard*

CHAPTER 1:

# NOTTINGHAM'S FIRST TRAMS:
# 61 YEARS OF SERVICE

**Above:** Track renewals appear to be taking place nearest the camera in this busy scene at Market Place as two trams are visible in the foreground and a third car can be seen in the background. *National Tramway Museum collection*

Nottingham's first generation tram network had its origins in the Nottingham Tramways Company, established in 1875 to operate horse tram services in the city. In 1877 the company was renamed the Nottingham & District Tramways Company, and on 17 September 1878 the first route opened between Trent Bridge and St Peter's Square in the city centre along with a branch serving the Great Northern Railway's London Road station (which was located adjacent to Midland station and is now used as a Virgin Active health club). Barely half a year later, on 5 April 1879, a third line was built between Market Place and Carrington Road, this route having no physical connection with the first two lines to open. Then on 11 August that year the Basford line opened from Market Place via Alfreton Road, Bentinck Road and Radford Road to Church Street gas works. A second pair of horses, known as trace horses or cock horses, was needed to pull the tram up the steep gradient on Derby Road.

### STEAM TRAM EXPERIMENT

In 1880 the company carried out trials with a steam tram from Messrs Hughes and Co from Loughborough. Then in 1885 Nottingham received its first (and only) steam tram loco, built by Wigan-based engineer William Wilkinson, and in the same year a top covered double deck bogie tram was purchased from Starbuck Car & Wagon Company in Birkenhead for use with the steam tram loco on the Basford route. However, this was not a success, as the steam tram cut only ten minutes off the 1h10 end-to-end journey time on this route. The steam tram loco was withdrawn just four years later in 1889, with the Starbuck car then being converted to a four-wheeled horse-drawn vehicle with its top cover removed, this car then being used on the Trent Bridge service for the rest of its days.

### HORSE TO ELECTRIC

During the horse tram era, the relationship between the tramway company and Nottingham Corporation was not an easy one. The tramway company announced proposals for extensions in November

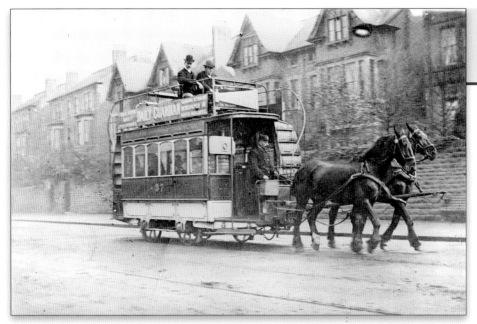

**Left:** One of the last horse trams to be built for Nottingham was car 37 constructed by G F Milnes & Co in 1895. It is seen heading along Mansfield Road bound for Carrington. *National Tramway Museum collection*

when many other operators of horse trams throughout the country were also seeking a more efficient replacement for horse-drawn traction. On 28 March that year the Tramways Committee of the Corporation recommended to the City Council that an overhead electric system should be used. City Engineer Arthur Brown and the Electrical Engineer then visited New York and Boston in the USA to carry out further investigations into the preferred car design and form of traction and current collection. They confirmed that an overhead system would have to be used although a conduit system involving current collection via a conduit running midway between the two running rails would be preferable.

Tenders for a new fleet of electric tramcars were invited from Westinghouse and Dick, Kerr & Company with that of Dick, Kerr & Co for 12 cars being accepted. The first nine electric trams were delivered to Nottingham in October 1900 and were assembled at Sherwood Depot. These were open-top four-wheelers with three windows in the lower deck saloon. A notable feature of these vehicles was that the staircases faced inwards instead of outwards. One car, No. 4, was completed by November and made a trial run from the depot into the city centre and back on 17 November that year carrying 3 tons of sand to represent a full payload of passengers.

Because the rest of the fleet had not been completed by December, a notice was served on Dick, Kerr & Co to complete them within seven days, and the work was duly done on them. The Dick Kerr cars were intended for the Sherwood route, on which services began on 1 January 1901. Meanwhile the Corporation placed an order with Westinghouse for ten cars for the Trent Bridge route. This was followed shortly afterwards by further orders for ten four-wheelers and ten bogie cars.

The Sherwood route was an immediate success from the start, with a fare of 2d being charged for the journey of just over two miles and trams operating every three minutes in peak hours and every five minutes off-peak. By 23 April 1901 new tracks had been laid along

1878, including lines to St Ann's Well Road and Bridge Street Radford, a link between the northern and southern sections along Wheeler Gate, and a connection from the end of Station Street via Plumtree Square onto the St Ann's Well Road route at Alfred Street South. These were rejected by the city council, but the tramway company was determined not to give up and so it submitted a fresh set of proposals for extensions to the council in November 1882 but these were again refused. At the next council meeting in January 1883 it was resolved that Nottingham Corporation should purchase the existing tramway lines on equitable terms and then build all further extensions itself, with the lines being leased to an operating company.

The existing tramways company had a 21-year licence to operate the network, however, and nothing more was done until 1890 when the directors of the Nottinghamshire and Midland Merchants' and Traders' Association complained to Nottingham Corporation that the existing tram service did not meet the needs of the city. They wanted to see a cheaper and quicker form of transport than horse trams.

In September 1896 Parliament agreed that the Corporation may apply to take over the operation of the tramway. On 14 June 1897 the Corporation purchased the tramway for £80 000, and on 18 October that year the network was handed over to the Corporation. All tramcars were then repainted in maroon & cream, and in 1899 the Nottingham Corporation Act was passed, which formalised the acquisition of the tram network by the Corporation.

Meanwhile in 1898 the Corporation sent a deputation to visit the cable tramway in Edinburgh and the overhead electric tram systems in Bristol and Dover to determine which method of propulsion would work best for Nottingham, at a time

**Right:** Car 22 at Canning Circus just west of Nottingham city centre. *H. Nicol/ National Tramway Museum collection*

**Left:** In 1911 car 129 was specially decorated for the coronation celebrations of King George V and Queen Mary. On one side, visible in this view, the bodyside bore the words "Long live the King" in lights (with the letters GR for George Rex beneath), and on the other side the words "Long live the Queen" with the letters MR for Mary Regina were carried. Here the special coronation tram is seen on Victoria Embankment on the north bank of the River Trent. *National Tramway Museum collection*

Wheeler Gate, connecting the northern and southern parts of the network for the first time. On 17 April horse trams started running from Gregory Boulevard over the new tracks to Bulwell Market; however, these were short-lived and were superseded by electric trams on 23 July after a trial run to Bulwell by car No. 13 on 8 July.

New routes to Lenton, St Ann's and Mapperley opened in 1902, and the last horse trams were withdrawn in the same year; then in 1903 a system of colour coding was introduced to enable passengers to tell where a car was travelling to, particularly at night as the destination boards (which were used rather than destination blinds as found on most other tramways) were not illuminated. The colours used (with those used on the side and front destination boards shown in brackets) were:

- Sherwood Station Street: red (white on red)
- Mapperley Trent Bridge: yellow (blue on yellow)
- St Ann's Well Road Boulevards: green (green on white)
- Nottingham Road Boulevards: blue (white on blue)
- Wilford Road Market Place: green (white on green)
- Bulwell Trent Bridge: red (red on white)
- Basford Market Place: white (white on black)

These colours were illuminated by a light in the lower saloon on the inside of the offside bulkhead, through which there was a circular hole so that this light could be seen from the outside. There were three coloured lenses on arms, which were pivoted and placed in front of the hole to show the appropriate colour.

Further extensions to Colwick Road and Wilford Road opened in 1907 for which ten new cars numbered 106 to 115 were purchased from Milnes Voss in Birkenhead. Unlike the existing fleet, these new vehicles had normal staircases and top-covered bodies. However, in April 1907 the Station Street–Colwick Road service was withdrawn after barely a month of operation. Instead a circular route was introduced from Colwick Road to Colwick Road via Station Street, the Market Place and Bath Street with cars running alternately in a clockwise and in an anticlockwise direction. This service likewise proved unprofitable and was withdrawn in October.

In 1908 the Corporation reached an agreement with the Nottinghamshire & Derbyshire Tramways Company for the construction of a line from the city centre to Cinderhill to connect with the existing lines at Basford, allowing for through connections. Then on 16 December 1910 a new route to Carlton Road opened, terminating at Thorneywood Lane (now known as Porchester Road). The same year also saw the last horse buses operating. Route numbers were introduced for the first time in 1912:

- Route 1: Sherwood–Trent Bridge
- Route 2: Mapperley–Trent Bridge
- Route 3: Bulwell–Trent Bridge
- Route 4: Basford–Colwick Road
- Route 5: Nottingham Road to Radford and Lenton
- Route 6: St Ann's Well Road to Radford and Lenton
- Route 7: Wilford Road–London Road
- Route 8: Carlton–Market Place

In 1915, route 9 was opened between Market Place, Arnold and Derby Road. This was the longest route on the system.

Staff shortages during World War I led to a significant reduction in vehicle maintenance standards, so large sums of money were earmarked for permanent way maintenance and the rebuilding of tramcar bodies after the war. In June 1917, over a year before the end of the war, an order was placed with United Electric Car Co Ltd for 12 replacement tramcar bodies and 35 sets of electrical equipment (including more powerful motors intended to replace the small motors fitted to the older cars) to be delivered as soon as circumstances allowed. By the end of the war it was realised that more trams would

**Right:** Notts & Derby car 12, with Nottingham Corporation car 106 just visible on the right. *H. Nicol/National Tramway Museum collection*

be needed to cater for increases in traffic so in 1919 25 four-wheel top covered cars were ordered from the English Electric Company, the successor to Dick Kerr & Co. The same company also built Nottingham's last first generation trams, a fleet of 20 fully enclosed cars delivered in 1926.

## THE NOTTS & DERBY

As well as the Nottingham Corporation Tramway network, Nottingham was also served by a short-lived interurban tram route linking the city with the Derbyshire market town of Ripley. This was operated by the Nottinghamshire & Derbyshire Tramways Company (commonly referred to as the Notts & Derby), which was formed in 1903 although the tram route itself did not open until 1913. The original Nottinghamshire & Derbyshire Tramways Company Bill of 1902 proposed a total of 79 miles (127 km) of track linking the tramway networks of Nottingham, Derby and Ilkeston. When passed the following year the Act only authorised the construction of 39 miles of route, of which only 11 miles were actually laid, the section from Ripley to Cinderhill in the north-west Nottingham suburbs.

The first section between Loscoe and Kimberley opened on 4 July that year, followed by the section to Cinderhill a month later and the rest of the route to Ripley on 1 January 1914. It then became possible to travel the 15 miles from Nottingham to Ripley by tram in 1h 40min. A mere 14 years after its completion, the Notts & Derby system suffered heavy losses, and this led the company to consider alternative forms of traction. In 1928 it promoted a parliamentary bill known as the Nottinghamshire & Derbyshire Traction Act 1928 to abandon the tramway system and replace it with trolleybuses. The company was then renamed the Nottinghamshire & Derbyshire Traction Co Ltd and the tramway closed as a through route on 31 December 1932, although a morning and evening workmen's service is said to have continued running between Cinderhill and Heanor until 6 October 1933 when the through trolleybus service started.

## DECLINE, CLOSURE AND TROLLEYBUS REPLACEMENT

It is often said that the heyday of tramways in the UK occurred between the 1900s and the 1920s, with the decline starting in the 1930s. After Wolverhampton in 1928 and Derby in 1934, Nottingham was the third major tramway closure in 1936 (although several small tram networks also closed during this period, including some in the East Midlands such as Chesterfield in 1927, Lincoln in 1929, and Mansfield in 1932).

The decision to replace the Notts & Derby system with trolleybuses came shortly before Nottingham Corporation Tramways General Manager John Aldworth retired. His successor W.G. Marks (former Manager of Chesterfield Corporation Transport) was appointed on 1 January 1929, and this led to a reappraisal of the transport undertaking whose name was changed to Nottingham Corporation Passenger Transport Department. Shortly after Mr Marks took over the leadership of the undertaking an order was placed for a large fleet of AEC motor buses, and at the same time the new manager suggested to the Transport Committee of Nottingham City Council that he be authorised to draw up a comprehensive plan to convert the tramway to trolleybus operation, the first trolleybuses having been introduced in 1927 on the route between the city centre and New Basford via Nottingham Road.

These plans were incorporated into the Nottingham Corporation Act 1930, which contained ambitious proposals to convert all tram routes and build lengthy trolleybus extensions to them. If these plans had been fully implemented, 200 trolleybuses would have been needed. In the event, although the scheme was passed in the House of Commons the routes that had not previously been served by trams were removed from the Bill by the House of Lords because of strong opposition from bus operator the Trent Motor Traction Company and Nottinghamshire County Council.

Despite the conversion of three tram routes to trolleybus in 1930, the tramcar fleet remained 200 strong with no vehicles being disposed

**Above:** Car 72 in Bulwell Market Place after arrival with a route 3 service from Trent Bridge. *National Tramway Museum collection*

of until 1931 when nine of the older cars were sold for £20 10s each. To distinguish tram services from bus and trolleybus services, in 1933 the remaining tram routes received letters instead of numbers:

- Route A: Mapperley–Trent Bridge (formerly route 2)
- Route B: Mapperley–Market Square (formerly route 2)
- Route C: Bulwell–Trent Bridge (formerly route 3)
- Route D: Basford–Colwick Road (formerly route 4)

**Above:** Car 192 is seen in Old Market Square on a route 1 service to Arnold in front of Nottingham's famous Council House, probably sometime in the late 1920s. This was one of the last batch of trams built for Nottingham by English Electric in 1926, 18 of which were sold to Aberdeen after closure of the Nottingham tramway in 1936. *M.J. O'Connor/National Tramway Museum collection*

**Left:** Car 159 passes through Old Market Square in Nottingham city centre on a route C (formerly route 3) service to Bulwell sometime between 1933 (when the remaining tram routes received letters instead of numbers) and closure of the system in 1936. *M.J. O'Connor/National Tramway Museum collection*

Manager of Aberdeen) had different ideas and favoured conversion of the remaining tram services to motor bus operation. Because of this, only three of the last seven surviving tram routes were converted to trolleybus. The last tram route to remain was the Arnold route, on which the last tram, car 190, ran on 5 September 1936, being driven to Parliament Street depot by the then Chairman of the Transport Committee, Alderman J. Farr JP and conducted by Inspector J.W. Vale who had also been the conductor on the first electric tram to run in Nottingham. Special tickets were issued for the final journey bearing the letters RIP in red. By the time car 190 reached the depot, souvenir hunters had taken just about everything that could be removed from the vehicle. 18 of the later 1926-built cars were then sold to Aberdeen Corporation, where they would remain in service until 1950.

- Route E: Villiers Road–Radford/Lenton (formerly route 6)
- Route F: London Road–Radford/Lenton (formerly route 7)
- Route H: Daybrook Square–Old Market Square (formerly part of route 1)
- Route J: LMS station–Colwick Road
- Route K: Arnold–Trent Bridge (formerly route 9)

The Carlton service had been intended to become route G, but had by this time been replaced by trolleybuses.

In 1934, Mr Marks was appointed as General Manager at Liverpool, and expressed regret at not being able to oversee the completion of the tramway conversion programme. His successor, J.L. Gunn (formerly

Meanwhile the Notts & Derby trolleybus service was withdrawn and replaced by motor buses in 1953 while the Nottingham Corporation trolleybuses continued to serve the city until 30 June 1966 when the last remaining route, via Nottingham Road, closed. This had also been the city's first trolleybus route in 1927 as mentioned above. A ceremonial last run then took place on the morning of 1 July 1966.

**Above:** A chance meeting of tram, trolleybus and motor bus sometime in 1934 or 1935. Car 181 heads onto Lower Parliament Street off King Edward Street with a route D (formerly route 4) service to Old Market Square, where route D (Colwick–Basford) had been cut back to terminate in May 1934 before being withdrawn completely in June 1935. An unidentified tram is just visible behind it, and alongside the two trams is AEC Reliance single deck bus No. 93, one of a batch of 20 delivered in 1929. This is followed by a new Ransome's three-axle trolleybus, one of the batch numbered 86–106. *National Tramway Museum collection*

## TRAM OR TROLLEYBUS?

Given that Nottingham was one of the first major cities in the UK to abandon its tramway in favour of trolleybuses it would seem appropriate to examine the advantages and disadvantages of trolleybuses compared to trams (and the pros and cons of both compared to motor buses). Indeed, when the present day Nottingham Express Transit light rail system was being planned and built in the 1990s and early 2000s some transport campaigners argued that a modern trolleybus system would have been a better solution for Nottingham than a tramway.

However, no trolleybus systems have existed in the UK (with the exception of those at museum sites) since the closure of the Bradford network in 1972 apart from a mile-long test route that briefly operated alongside Doncaster Racecourse in the mid-1980s with a view to reintroducing trolleybuses on four bus routes in Doncaster and two in Rotherham (a plan that never came to fruition, partly as a result of bus deregulation in 1986). An Alexander RH-bodied Dennis Dominator was converted to a trolleybus for this experiment, and is now preserved at Sandtoft (see below).

More recently, two other UK cities have also proposed but abandoned plans for trolleybus systems. In the 1990s Merseytravel Passenger Transport Executive proposed a guided trolleybus route known as the Mersey Rapid Transit linking Liverpool city centre with Page Moss in the city's eastern suburbs but this scheme was rejected at public inquiry. In response, Merseytravel proposed a three-line tram network known as Merseytram (which itself was finally abandoned on cost

grounds in 2013 having previously been cancelled in 2005). Ironically, unlike many other major UK cities, Liverpool had never previously had trolleybuses.

Meanwhile Metro PTE proposed a trolleybus system for Leeds in 2007 in response to the Department for Transport's rejection of the Leeds Supertram proposal in 2005 on cost grounds. This project, known as the Leeds New Generation Transport (NGT) scheme, would have consisted of routes from the city centre to the north, south and east of the city. The DfT approved the South route from Holt Park to Stourton in 2012, and this was followed by a public inquiry in 2014. However, a negative report from the public inquiry led to the NGT scheme being cancelled in 2016, despite Leeds being the biggest city in Western Europe without any form of mass transit system (although a new mass transit scheme for West Yorkshire was promised as part of the Department for Transport's Integrated Rail Plan published in November 2021, shortly before this book went to press).

Although the cost of installing the necessary infrastructure for a trolleybus system would have been cheaper and the amount of disruption during construction work on the street sections would have been much less than for a tramway (see below), if such a network had followed similar or identical alignments to the present day NET network, guided busways would have been needed on the off-street sections.

**Above:** Trolleybus 44 is seen on Middleton Boulevard on a route 9 service to Carlton in 1932. This was part of a batch of 13 vehicles delivered in 1932 with Brush H32/28R bodywork and a Ransomes Sims & Jefferies D6 chassis. *British Trolleybus Society collection*

### Trolleybuses: advantages compared to trams

- Easier traffic avoidance and greater operational flexibility: Trams are completely fixed in the route that they follow and cannot run where there are no tracks or dodge around other road users or parked vehicles, whereas a trolleybus can manoeuvre around obstacles. Trolleybuses can also be moved to the side of the road and their trolley poles lowered when not in service, and if fitted with a small diesel engine or battery motor can also run on roads not equipped with trolleybus overhead wires if necessary.
- Easier driver training: Because the technique for driving and controlling a trolleybus is similar to that of a conventional bus, the potential staff pool for operating all types of bus (trolleybuses and motor buses) is much greater than for trams.
- Cheaper infrastructure: The need for rails, signals and other infrastructure means that the initial start-up cost of trams is much higher. The need to divert the utilities under the streets when building a tramway and the disruption associated with this work is avoided when building a trolleybus system. Trolleybuses can pull over to the kerb like conventional buses, meaning that no special boarding platforms at the roadside or in the middle of the road are needed so trolleybus stops can more easily be moved as required.
- Quietness*: Trolleybuses are quieter than either trams or motor buses. However, although it is desirable to reduce noise levels, especially in residential areas, this has also led to the criticism that trolleybuses are often so quiet that you can hardly hear them coming, which can lead to passengers missing them and other road users getting hit and injured or even killed by them. Trams are also generally quieter than motor buses.
- Better hill climbing*: The rubber tyres on trolleybuses have better adhesion than trams' steel wheels on steel rails, making them better for hill climbing and braking. Trolleybuses are also

better than motor buses on hilly routes because electric motors offer much higher static torque when starting up. Electric motors use power from a central plant and can be overloaded for short periods without damage unlike internal combustion engines.

### Advantages compared to motor buses

Apart from the advantages marked * above, which apply to trolleybuses compared to both trams and motor buses, trolleybuses also offer the following advantages compared to motor buses (all of these also apply to trams compared to motor buses):

- Environmentally friendly: Trams and trolleybuses are more environmentally friendly than vehicles that run on fossil fuels or hydrocarbon-based fuels because electrically powered vehicles do not emit greenhouse gases when in motion. Electricity from a centralised power plant is often produced more efficiently. Trolleybuses are especially favoured where electricity is cheap, abundant and renewable, such as hydroelectric power. Trolleybuses and trams can generate power from kinetic energy while braking, a process known as regenerative braking. Another tram or trolleybus on the same circuit can then make use of the electricity generated in that way. The use of trams or trolleybuses also eliminates pollution when standing at a stop or at a signal or traffic light.
- Usable in enclosed spaces: The lack of exhaust allows trams and trolleybuses to operate underground. No UK trolleybus system ever operated underground, and the only first generation UK tramway to feature a tunnel section was the Kingsway Subway in London. At present the only UK tramway tunnel section (if it can be classed as such) is Piccadilly station undercroft on Manchester's Metrolink network, although the Tyne & Wear Metro runs in tunnels beneath Newcastle city centre and the Bank branch of the Docklands Light Railway runs underground. In mainland Europe and some other parts of the

world, tramways or light rail systems operating in tunnels are commonplace, and there are also several examples of trolleybus tunnels such as in Cambridge, Massachusetts, USA, and on the two trolleybus systems in Japan: Kurobe Dam and Tateyama, Toyama. The Downtown Seattle Transit Tunnel in Seattle, USA, is used by both trolleybuses and light rail vehicles.

- Longevity and maintenance: Electric motors are more durable than internal combustion engines, with less secondary damage from vibration, so trams and electric buses tend to have a longer life expectancy than motor buses.
- Higher capacity per vehicle, at least in the case of trams and articulated trolleybuses compared to conventional single decker buses (although this also applies to articulated or double deck motor buses to some extent), meaning that fewer vehicles are needed to carry the same number of passengers, congestion is lower and staff productivity higher.

### Disadvantages compared to trams

All of these disadvantages also apply to motor buses compared to trams.

- Less attractive to potential passengers: For many years the bus has been perceived by many motorists as a form of transport that people only use if they have to, and at least in the UK this applies even to glorified bus-based systems such as guided busways/"bus rapid transit" systems. Research and evidence has shown that no form of bus-based system will attract motorists out of their cars, but trams and other forms of rail-based system will.
- More control needed: Trolleybuses have to be driven in a similar manner to motor buses, requiring directional control by the driver.
- Less efficient use of right of way: Lanes have to be wider for unguided buses than for trams, as unguided buses can drift from side to side whereas trams can safely run on parallel tracks and can pass closer together than bus or trolleybus drivers could safely steer.
- Higher rolling resistance: Rubber-tyred vehicles have more rolling resistance (i.e. the force resisting the motion when an object such as a wheel rolls on a surface) than steel wheels, and this reduces energy efficiency.
- Problems with platform loading: Level platform loading with only a minimal gap between the platform and the vehicle is easier and cheaper to implement with rail vehicles whether at design stage or afterwards.

### Disadvantages compared to motor buses

All of these disadvantages also apply to some extent to trams compared to motor buses.

- Difficult or impossible to reroute: If no other route with wires (and tracks in the case of trams) is available, whenever a tram or trolleybus route has to be temporarily closed it is less easy or impossible to find a diversionary route than for motor buses. In the case of trams,

replacement bus services often have to be provided instead. This can also happen with trolleybuses if the vehicles do not have a small diesel engine or battery motor for operating away from the wires, or they may have to be diverted via a longer and more circuitous route so that they can stay under the wires.

- Aesthetics: Overhead wires can be visually intrusive especially in the case of trolleybus wires, which consist of two wires alongside each other. Because of this, intersections often consist of multiple crossing and converging sets of wires, resulting in a "webbed junction" appearance.
- Higher capital cost of equipment: Although trolleybuses have a longer life expectancy than motor buses, market demand is limited because of the much lower number of trolleybus systems than motor bus networks. This means that the price of a trolleybus is generally higher than for a motor bus.
- Inability to overtake other trolleybuses: Unlike motor buses, trolleybuses cannot overtake each other in regular service except in the case of vehicles with off-wire capability or where two parallel sets of wires with a switch are provided.
- Dewirement: Trolley poles sometimes come off the wire, although such occurrences are relatively rare on modern systems with well maintained infrastructure. Trolleybuses have special insulated pole ropes that drivers use to reconnect the trolley poles with the overhead wires.
- More training needed: Trolleybus drivers need to learn how to prevent dewiring, slowing down at turns and when running through switches in the wires, for example. The need to decelerate in such instances can also potentially add slightly to traffic congestion.
- Overhead wires create obstruction: Where trolleybuses or trams share road space with other vehicles, the wires can limit the maximum height of tall vehicles such as lorries and double-deck buses and coaches that may wish to use or cross roads equipped with trolleybus or tram wires. This is less likely to have been an issue in the days of double-deck trolleybuses, which were the norm on most of the UK trolleybus networks; however, no double-deck trolleybuses have operated in normal service anywhere in the world since the end of 1997 when the trolleybus system in Porto, Portugal, closed. All of the world's remaining trolleybus systems use only single-deck vehicles and often have overhead wires that are only high enough for single-deck trolleybuses. That said, some modern tramways such as Sheffield Supertram do have overhead wires that are high enough to accommodate double-deck buses even if the trams themselves are all single-deck.

**Right:** Trolleybus 480 negotiates its way around the turning circle at Ransome Road terminus on Wells Road on a route 47 service on 8 August 1963, two years before most of the trolleybus network closed with the exception of the route via Nottingham Road which would last until 1966. This was one of a batch of four vehicles delivered in 1948 with Roe H30/26R bodywork and a Karrier W chassis. *Tony Belton*

It is also worth noting that advances in battery technology could substantially reduce the cost of new light rail lines and systems if the current Very Light Rail experiment in the West Midlands proves successful, and could also put the long-term future of trolleybuses in doubt as these could increasingly disappear in favour of electric buses that are recharged at charging points (in the same way as electric cars) or hybrid electric buses that use a combination of a conventional diesel engine and an electric propulsion system. The use of bio-fuels also reduces the environmental impact of motor buses.

Wellington, New Zealand, had a trolleybus network from 1949 until 2017. The system was then controversially abandoned and initially replaced by conventional diesel buses (albeit compliant with Euro 5 emission standards) but these are now being progressively superseded by electric buses with all of the city's buses planned to be electric by 2030.

## PRESERVED NOTTINGHAM TRAMS AND TROLLEYBUSES

Unfortunately there are currently no first generation Nottingham trams in fully restored condition; indeed, it is lucky that any vehicles were saved (even if they are in incomplete and unrestored condition) given that the city's tramway closed earlier than those of many other major UK cities. The lower body of car 45, built by Dick, Kerr & Co in 1901, survives and was moved from the Nottingham Heritage Railway (formerly the Great Central Railway – Nottingham or Nottingham Transport Heritage Centre) at Ruddington to the National Tramway Museum (a.k.a. Crich Tramway Village) in November 2018. It is currently in storage on site at Crich and not on public display. In the

long term it is envisaged that the lower body of car 45 could form part of a display about grounded tram bodies but there are no firm plans to progress this project at present.

The other three surviving Nottingham trams form part of the National Tramway Museum collection but are stored at an off-site storage facility and thus not accessible to the public: Dick Kerr car 92 built in 1902, United Electric Car Co car 121 built in 1908, and English Electric car 166 built in 1920. Only one cab end of car 121 survives, making this one an unlikely candidate for restoration, while only the lower bodies of cars 92 and 166 remain in existence. After withdrawal from service in 1934, car 92 was dismantled and its lower body (minus fittings and truck) was sold to become a holiday letting at a static caravan park in Torksey, Lincolnshire, where it remained until 1985. It was initially acquired by the Nottingham Industrial Museum but was then passed on to the National Tramway Museum when the scale of the restoration that would be required became apparent. Similarly the lower body of car 166 was sold for conversion to a bungalow at a farm where it remained until 2007. Cars 92 and 166 are both seen as possible long-term restoration projects.

Six Nottingham trolleybuses have been preserved, four of which are at the Trolleybus Museum at Sandtoft near Doncaster. Of these, vehicles 493 and 506 are in working order and 367 and 466 are undergoing restoration at the time of writing. Sandtoft is also the home of Notts & Derby trolleybus 353, which is currently stored off-site awaiting restoration. Sandtoft also owns the chassis of Nottingham 46 (latterly numbered 346). The other two surviving Nottingham trolleybuses form part of a private collection.

**Below:** Appropriately adorned with "City of Nottingham Last Trolleybus" decals, trolleybus 506 poses with the Mayor of Nottingham on the occasion of its ceremonial last run on 1 July 1966, the day after the last public runs of the city's trolleybuses. This was one of a number of batches delivered in 1948–52 with Brush bodywork and a BUT964IT chassis. Vehicle 506 is now preserved at Sandtoft (see photo, facing page). *Tony Belton*

**Above:** The lower body of car 92 at the National Tramway Museum's off-site storage facility. It is very similar to that of car 45, which the museum acquired in 2018. *Jim Dignan*

**Above:** The lower body of car 166. *Jim Dignan*

**Above:** The surviving cab end of car 121. *Jim Dignan*

### USEFUL WEBSITES

- British Trolleybus Society: *www.britishtrolley.org.uk*
- British Trolleybuses database: *www.trolleybus.co.uk*
- Crich Tramway Village: *www.tramway.co.uk*
- The Trolleybus Museum at Sandtoft: *https://sandtoft.org*

**Below:** Superbly restored trolleybus 506 at Sandtoft museum. *Tony Wilson*

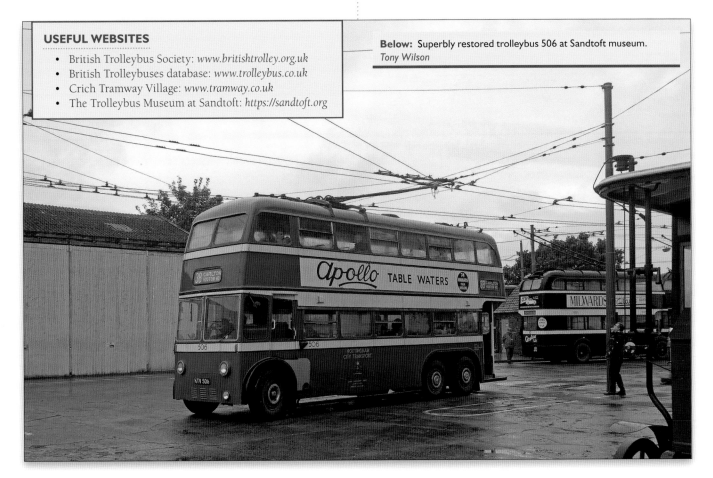

**CHAPTER 2:**

# TRAMWAY REVIVAL

**Above:** Bulwell tram stop under construction on 19 May 2003 as unit 156 410, forming a Robin Hood Line service, calls at the heavy rail station, which has been reduced to a single platform to accommodate the tram tracks. *Mike Haddon*

After the closure of Nottingham's trolleybus system in 1966, for the next 38 years the city's public transport offering would consist solely of motor buses and a very limited network of local rail services. Ironically, as early as 1911 competition from the city's tram network had led to the closure of Lenton station on the now reopened Midland Railway route to Mansfield. This was followed in 1916 by the three intermediate stations on the Nottingham Suburban Railway at Sherwood, St Ann's Well and Thorneywood in the eastern part of the city for the same reason.

Fast forward nearly half a century and in 1960 the former Great Northern line between Colwick and Basford via Gedling and Daybrook closed to passengers. Four years later, 1964 saw the withdrawal of the Nottingham–Mansfield–Worksop rail service as part of the Beeching inspired closure programme, leaving Mansfield as one of the UK's largest towns without its own railway station. However, the line remained open for freight and would reopen to passengers in stages during the 1990s when it was christened the Robin Hood Line: Nottingham–Newstead reopened in 1993, Newstead–Mansfield Woodhouse in 1995 and then trains ran through to Worksop in 1998.

Other significant post-war rail closures included the Great Central Main Line between Nottingham and Sheffield in 1966 and the remaining stub of the GCML between Nottingham and Rugby in 1969, both of which further reduced the size of the local network. Following the closure of Nottingham Victoria station in 1967 the remaining token Nottingham–Rugby local service had been truncated at Nottingham Arkwright Street station.

In the 1960s Nottingham had ambitious plans to boost its importance as a regional shopping centre, hence the construction of the Victoria Centre shopping complex and bus station on the former Victoria station site (where the old Victoria station clock tower remains as the sole surviving part of the station). At around the same time public transport surveys found that the largest numbers of passengers were being carried on bus routes serving the north and north-west of the city and on routes to the south via the Trent bridges. It is probably no coincidence that these areas would be selected for the first two phases of the present day tram network.

This was followed by the Broadmarsh shopping centre and bus station in the early 1970s, located close to Nottingham Midland station and the former Great Central viaduct. Meanwhile, 1966 saw the publication of a highway plan entitled Traffic in Nottingham 1965–2000, which proposed a network of new roads around the city. However, in the event the only one of these schemes to be implemented was the A6008 Maid Marian Way around the western edge of the city centre. The other new road plans were abandoned, largely because of public opposition, and in 1972 a free bus service linking the Broadmarsh and Victoria centres was introduced. This coincided with the announcement by Nottingham City Council of a new transport policy with an emphasis on pedestrianisation, limiting car use, and improvements to public transport.

In the May 1974 edition of Light Rail Transit Association's Modern Tramway (now Tramways & Urban Transit) magazine, the well known railway and tramway enthusiast and writer John Price (1926–98) wrote an article proposing to reuse the former Great Central Railway tunnels beneath Nottingham city centre as part of a modern rapid transit system. He suggested that "Car parks could be built at Cinderhill and Bulwell with electric trains through New Basford to a station in the disused railway cutting at Victoria Station North, facing the new bus station." However, this scheme never saw the light of day, and much of the former GC route was subsequently built over.

Then in 1987 Nottingham Development Enterprise (NDE), a public/private partnership involving Nottingham City and Nottinghamshire County Councils, was set up. A report by NDE in February 1989 recommended a light rail system with an initial line using part of the former Great Central Railway alignment between the city centre and Hucknall with a branch over a former colliery line to Cinderhill, now the site of the Phoenix Park Business Park. NDE also carried out a feasibility study in the same year that showed such a line to be technically possible. In the longer term NDE envisaged a network also consisting of a city centre loop via Wilkinson Street and lines serving Toton in the south-west and Gedling in the east.

The City Council rejected NDE's original proposal involving use of the ex-GC tunnel from Victoria but accepted an on-street alternative via Waverley Street, Goldsmith Street, Market Street, Old Market Square, Victoria Street and Weekday Cross. The Parliamentary Bill for the lines serving Hucknall and Cinderhill gained Royal Assent in July 1994. In the early 1990s NDE had proposed to share the heavy rail tracks between Wilkinson Street and Hucknall but this was found not to be practicable. The concept of light rail vehicles and conventional heavy rail trains sharing the same tracks had already been tried and proven to work in Nottingham's German twin city of Karlsruhe where "tram-train" operation over heavy rail routes physically connected to the city's tram network had started in 1991, providing direct services into the city centre without the need to change modes en route.

However, this type of operation was then unknown in the UK and a number of technical issues would have needed to be overcome, such as devising a signalling system compatible with both types of vehicle, accommodating separately managed services on the same tracks, and the differing platform heights needed for high-floor heavy rail trains and low-floor trams. Two potential solutions to the platform height issue could have been to use high-floor light rail vehicles and standard height platforms at all tram stops (as on Manchester's Metrolink tram network) or to provide low platforms for the trams or tram-trains and standard height platforms for conventional trains at each stop that was served by both modes (as at Rotherham Central station to cater for the South Yorkshire tram-train, which opened in 2018).

NDE's studies in the early 1990s found that the cost of construction could be reduced by opting for shared heavy and light rail operation on the same tracks, especially if this would eliminate the need for new structures and expensive land acquisition. However, it was also found that operational costs would be greater, and the uncertainties regarding privatisation meant that private sector operators would have had to take on the unknown costs and liabilities involved for which there was no clear precedent anywhere in the UK. Because of this, a completely self-contained network rather than shared tracks eventually won the day, with the Phase 1 route to Hucknall and Phoenix Park running alongside the Robin Hood Line but not sharing the same tracks.

A number of alternative route options were considered for the Phase 1 route, including:

**Above:** Track laying is in progress on the new viaduct carrying the section of tramway from Middle Hill to Nottingham Midland station as seen on 31 August 2002. In the background can be seen the former High Pavement Chapel, now the Pitcher & Piano pub. Note the banner giving a projected opening date of November 2003. That target date was not met! *Mike Haddon*

- Reusing the ex-GCR viaduct and tunnels from Midland station via the site of the former Victoria station to a point near the north end of the Mansfield Road tunnel, where the line would have emerged via a new exit ramp and then taken a sharp left turn onto Gregory Boulevard, running alongside the Forest Recreation Ground. At the junction with Noel Street, close to the site of the present day tram stop at The Forest, the line would have turned right onto Noel Street and then followed the route that was eventually chosen including the separate northbound and southbound alignments via Noel Street and Radford Road respectively.

- Running as far as The Forest as now but then turning left onto Gregory Boulevard and Alfreton Road, then running alongside the Robin Hood Line from Bobber's Mill, rejoining the present day alignment at a point just north of the current Wilkinson Street stop.

- Alternative routes from Middle Hill, just north of Midland station, to the Old Market Square involving combinations of single unidirectional tracks via Low Pavement and either Wheeler Gate or Pelham Street.

Reusing the former GCR alignment would have meant omitting the Old Market Square, the Royal Centre and Nottingham Trent University, all of which are important sources of traffic. New residential developments on former railway land over the years at locations such as Bagthorpe, New Basford and Sherwood Rise effectively ruled out reusing the former GCR alignment north of Carrington station near the junction of Mansfield Road and Gregory Boulevard.

The disused GCR tunnels that had served Victoria station were still in fairly good condition by the 1990s, except that water ingress had led to the deterioration of Victoria Street tunnel to the south of the former Victoria station. At the Victoria station site itself a diversionary tunnel around or beneath the Victoria Centre would have been needed if the former GCR route through the city centre were to be used, as the columns in the car park area supporting the shopping complex and apartment block would have precluded the use of the original route. Such a tunnel was initially estimated to cost around £12 million to build, and the 1987 King's Cross Underground station fire had led to the introduction of new regulations for underground railway or light rail stations. This would have made such installations more costly and complex, and would probably only have allowed one city centre

stop to be provided.

The tunnels to the north and south of the former Victoria station site remained largely intact and unused for many years until the tunnel section to the south of the Victoria Centre was eventually used for district heating pipes running from a waste incinerator on the former Cattle Market site. Then in 2007, after the NET Phase 1 routes had opened, work started on the new Centre for Contemporary Art (now known as Nottingham Contemporary), which was built against the south portal of the tunnel, just south of Lace Market tram stop. The new art gallery was completed in 2009. All of this put paid to the idea of reusing the former GCR route apart from a very short section between Lace Market and Midland station.

## PROMOTING THE PROJECT

In 1991 NDE and the city and county councils set up a joint venture company entitled Greater Nottingham Rapid Transit Ltd to promote the NET project and take it through its development stage. In November of that year the Nottingham Light Rapid Transit Bill was deposited in Parliament and received the Royal Assent on 21 July 1994, the same day that the Croydon Tramlink Act was passed. NET and Croydon Tramlink (now London Trams) were the last completely new tram networks in England to be approved using the Private Bill procedure, which dated back to the 19th century but would be superseded by the Transport and Works Act 1992 for all future light rail schemes.

On 3 December 1998 Minister of State for Transport Dr John Reid announced the Government's formal approval for NET and their £167 million funding contribution secured through a Private Finance Initiative (PFI), thus enabling the City Council to finalise a full financial package for the scheme. Dr Reid said it was the Government's view that future light rail projects should be financed using revenue from congestion and parking charges, but also warned that "NET will take up a large part of my Department's allocation of resources...over the next few years. We will not be in a position to support similar schemes for the foreseeable future." He hoped that greater devolution to the English regions, as well as to London, Scotland, Wales and Northern Ireland, would remedy this situation, but in the event the 1997–2010 Labour Government's proposal for elected regional assemblies was not implemented following the "no" vote in a referendum in the North-East on 4 November 2004. Since then the lack of devolved regional government in England (with the exception of London) has been partially addressed by the creation of Combined Authorities for some areas of the country.

Despite this, to date NET has been the most recent completely new light rail system to open in England with only one more tramway in the UK having opened in Edinburgh, the Scottish capital, in 2014. It should also be noted that NET is so far the only light rail scheme in England that is not in an area covered by a Passenger Transport Executive, although Edinburgh also has no PTE.

during June and July 2003. The wires were suspended from buildings where possible to reduce the number of poles. Meanwhile, work on the depot site at Wilkinson Street started as early as 2001 and 20 January 2003 was a landmark day, with the overhead wires within the depot energised for the first time, and the first tram moved under its own power a week later. Car 202 moved outside the depot on 2 March that year, and two weeks later on 16 March cars 201 and 207 ran between Wilkinson Street and David Lane Crossing.

Since the opening of NET Phase 1 at least three proposed English light rail schemes have been abandoned: Liverpool's Merseytram in 2005 (which was then revived in 2008, only to be definitively cancelled in 2013 as mentioned in chapter 1) and Leeds Supertram, also in 2005. The Bristol Supertram project was cancelled in 2004, the same year that NET Phase 1 opened; however, in July 2021 the Transport for Greater Bristol Alliance and zero carbon campaign group Zero West published a pre-feasibility study setting out fresh proposals for a light rail network serving Bristol and Bath.

## CONSTRUCTION UNDER WAY

Construction of the new tramway started in June 2000, and by August of that year part of the old Great Central viaduct near the since closed Broadmarsh shopping centre and bus station was being demolished. By early 2001 work on its replacement structure that would carry the tramway was well advanced. Meanwhile on the street sections utility diversion work was well underway, along with the clearing of undergrowth alongside the Robin Hood Line towards Bulwell and on the former freight railway alignment to Cinderhill.

The first on-street tracks were laid in Noel Street in the Hyson Green area on 26 November 2001 and was followed by track laying in the Arboretum area. Track laying started in Nottingham city centre in February 2002 and had reached the Old Market Square by December 2002, two months after the first trams arrived in October of that year. Poles and wires were installed on the first city centre sections

**Right:** Construction work in progress in Fletcher Gate at the site of the future Lace Market stop on 20 April 2002. The section over the former Great Central Railway alignment towards Midland station is just behind the camera. *Mike Haddon (2)*

**Above:** Track laying in progress in Market Street looking towards the Old Market Square on 31 August 2002.
*Mike Haddon*

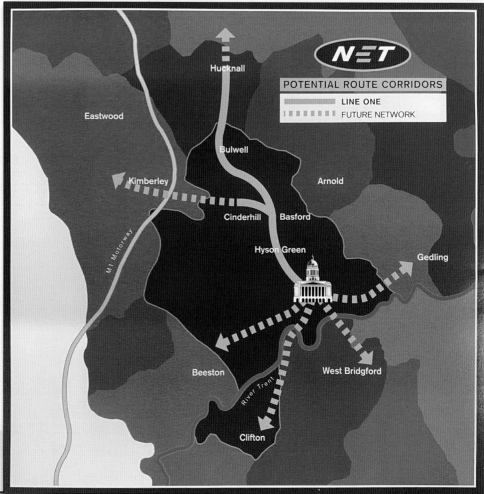

**Right:** An illustration of potential route corridors that could be served by NET in the future in an "Introducing NET" leaflet of March 2001.

**Above:** Track laying in progress in Noel Street on 20 April 2002. Here the northbound track continues straight ahead as the southbound track curves off to the left.

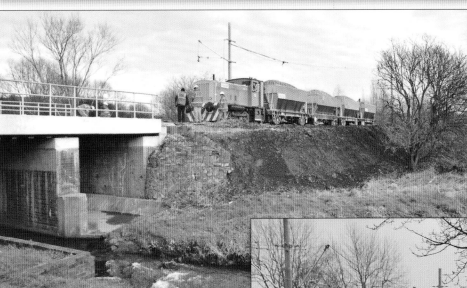

**Left:** A Grant Rail ballast train approaches the bridge over the River Leen on the Phoenix Park branch on 18 January 2003.

**Right:** An unidentified Bombardier Incentro tram on a test run passes 156 415 on a Robin Hood Line service near David Lane, running alongside the River Leen at this point, on 24 March 2003. *Mike Haddon (3)*

**Above:** The junction for the Phoenix Park branch at Highbury Vale is seen under construction on 18 January 2003, with the ballast train on site.

**Left:** A disused railway trackbed was used for much of the branch to Phoenix Park. This view looking east on 31 August 2002 shows how one of the bridge holes of the Cinderhill Road overbridge is being reused for its original purpose. The Cinderhill tram stop is located around the curve just beyond the bridge.

**Right:** Bulwell tram stop under construction on 31 August 2002 as hybrid unit 156 409, formed of a Class 153 single unit (nearest the camera) and a Class 156 driving car from 156 409, calls at the heavy rail station, which has been reduced to a single platform to accommodate the tram tracks. *Mike Haddon (3)*

## DELAY TO OPENING

The system was originally targeted to open on 11 November 2003, but in July 2003 Arrow Light Rail Ltd and the contractor, the Bombardier Carillion Consortium, said it needed longer than anticipated to carry out commissioning, testing and staff training and to find suitable sub-contractors and material suppliers. Technical problems during test runs also required some adjustments to track and poles, and a derailment occurred at Highbury Vale (Phoenix Park platforms) during initial tests in May 2003. The accident was understood to have been caused by faulty points. The opening was initially pushed back to January 2004 and later to "early spring"; the second delay was said to be mainly down to a shortage of skilled contractors and materials (such as stone paving slabs), hold ups in street lighting installation, adjustments needed to track and pointwork to enable trams to run at higher speeds and some issues with the alignment of trams and platform edges.

Driver training got under way between the depot at Wilkinson Street and the Phoenix Park terminus from March 2003 and there were several milestones during that summer. On 6 July 2003 car 210 became the first tram to reach both Bulwell and Hucknall under its own power, initially on test at low speed and then on a

**Above:** 209 is seen at David Lane on a test run on the Hucknall line on 24 March 2003.

series of test runs at line speed. 20 July 2003 saw the first tram run on the on-street sections on the outskirts of Nottingham city centre – in the early hours car 214 moved from the depot to The Forest stop. The early hours of 9 September 2003 saw the first tram run into Nottingham city centre, almost exactly 67 years to the day since the last tram in the city. Starting at 05.00 car 208 made a number of test runs between Basford and the railway station,

**Above:** 204 arrives at The Forest on a southbound test run on 30 September 2003. *Mike Haddon (2)*

**Above:** 204 makes a brief call at Wilkinson Street on a southbound "ghost run" on 18 February 2004.

**Right:** An unidentified Incentro tram calls at Shipstone Street on the northbound single line between The Forest and Wilkinson Street during "ghost running" on 18 February 2004.
*Mike Haddon (2)*

Some original NET leaflets.

**Above:** The invited guests look on as trams 205 (left) and 211 (right) pause in Old Market Square during the official opening of NET Phase 1.

**Right:** 215 (left) and 202 (right) are seen at the then Station Street terminus on 8 March 2004, the day of the NET Phase 1 official opening. *Alan Yearsley (3)*

**Left:** On the first day of public operation, 9 March 2004, a Hucknall bound tram calls at Highbury Vale as a Robin Hood Line Class 170, then operated by Central Trains, speeds north towards Worksop. The Phoenix Park branch can be seen diverging to the right.

**Below:** 204 runs into the Shipstone Street stop with a Phoenix Park service on the first day of public operation. *Peter Fox (2)*

pausing for photographs at around 07.00 in Old Market Square. This meant that by this stage trams had operated over the whole of the Phase 1 system. Further test runs took place in the following weeks.

Ahead of the opening, in early January 2004 "ghost running" started, involving operating the initial timetable but without passengers.

## OFFICIAL OPENING

NET Phase 1 was officially opened on 8 March 2004 by Transport Secretary Alistair Darling in the presence of the Lord Mayor of Nottingham and a number of other local dignitaries. The Transport Secretary arrived at the Town Hall (a.k.a. Council House) on car 205 at 10.30 and was met by Nottingham MPs Alan Simpson and John Heppell. Because of capacity constraints caused by the single line sections, trams did not run to Hucknall or Phoenix Park on this day. After the last of the guests had returned to the city centre from Bulwell, the trams reverted to "ghost running" to their booked times but without passengers.

The next day, 9 March, was the first day of normal service. Incentro tram 203 formed the first public working, leaving Phoenix Park at 05.58 carrying a large number of enthusiasts, staff, and members of the press. This was followed by car 214 on the 06.02 from Hucknall. Unsurprisingly on this day all trams were heavily loaded, meaning that the trams could not keep time because of the large numbers of people boarding and alighting at each stop. Unfortunately, the first day of public operation was marred by the failure of the level crossing at David Lane at 16.50. This crossing has barriers for the heavy rail line and traffic signals for the tramway. Train services were not disrupted as the barriers were stuck in the down position; however, the traffic signals, including the tram signals, did not show a proceed aspect, meaning that the trams were held up for around 50 minutes before a police officer was able to attend. Despite this, the first day of public

service on 9 March 2004 was reported to have seen more than over 40 000 people using the trams.

NET started with around 170 staff; this included 35 conductors after it was decided that conductors would be used on each tram, at least initially.

## TOWARDS PHASE 2

Even before the Phase 1 network opened, in late 2001 NET conducted a public consultation in the areas to be served by the Phase 2 routes. Two possible routes were considered for the Toton Lane route, via the Queens Medical Centre or via the Boots headquarters site to the south of the Midland Main Line between Nottingham and Beeston stations.

Two variants of the Boots option were also considered for the Beeston Rylands area adjacent to Beeston station, via Lilac Grove or alongside the existing heavy rail line between Beeston station and Humber Road South. In Chilwell, an alignment continuing straight along High Road and then taking a sharp right turn onto Cator Lane was considered as an alternative to the route via Brookland Drive and the Central College site which was eventually chosen.

**Left:** The second section of the new bridge to carry the Phase 2 lines over Nottingham Midland station, later to be named the Karlsruhe Friendship Bridge, was under construction just south of the station on 30 March 2013, prior to being lowered into position.

In the University of Nottingham area, as an alternative to the chosen route via University Boulevard the route could have run via the north side of the university campus. Five different variants of the via QMC option were considered for the Beeston area, including options via Queens Road, Regent Street/Broadgate, and Middle Street/Fletcher Road (the chosen option).

A number of options were also considered for the Clifton South route. These included a route running close to the A453 Queens Drive on the west side of the River Trent as an alternative to the chosen route via Wilford on the east side of the Trent. An alignment to the west of the Trent would have followed a short section of the same route as the Toton Lane line if the Boots option for this route had also been chosen instead of the QMC option. Both the

**Below:** The ramp leading to Nottingham station bridge is seen under construction on 26 July 2013.

**Below:** Track work in progress on Nottingham station bridge on 19 May 2014. *Mike Haddon (3)*

(the latter was known as the "Chilwell Line" for many years). The two councils then voted on 22 February and 3 March 2007 respectively to submit a Transport & Works Act Order application. The NET Phase 2 Transport & Works Act Order was given by the Government on 30 March 2009; however, following the 2009 elections the County Council was no longer willing to fund the project so the City Council decided to make up the shortfall (funded by money raised from a controversial workplace parking levy) and became the sole promoter of Phase 2, for which Government approval was received on 31 July 2009 by the then Transport Minister Sadiq Khan during a visit to the city. The Government would provide PFI credits capped at £530.7 million towards the £680 million cost of the scheme, with the city being responsible for finding £149 million through the workplace parking levy, and the shortfall being made up by £13 million of additional PFI credits. The parking levy also supported the £67 million redevelopment of Nottingham railway station.

Boots option for the Toton Lane line and the Queens Drive option for the Clifton South line would have involved longer journey times and higher construction and running costs but would also have required less private land acquisition and had a lesser ecological impact along the route. In both cases the chosen routes via QMC and Wilford were also found to be better value for money and were expected to generate higher numbers of passengers.

Three different route options via Wilford were also considered: apart from the chosen alignment via part of the former Great Central Railway route, the other variants involved using a short section of the old railway alignment and then Wilford Lane and Ruddington Lane, or continuing along Main Road and Ruddington Lane.

### PHASE 2 GETS GO-AHEAD

Following the opening of the Phase 1 routes, on 25 October 2006 the Government agreed to provide up to £437 million in Private Finance Initiative (PFI) credits, with Nottinghamshire County and Nottingham City Councils also providing up to £141 million in PFI credits for the Phase 2 routes to Clifton South and Toton

Following the 2010 General Election the scheme survived the 2010 Comprehensive Spending Review, with funding for NET Phase 2 being confirmed by the Government on 24 March 2011. However, after the spending review the Government cut its funding from 75% to 66% with the city council's contribution rising from 25% to 33%. The Department for Transport's first payment would be a maximum of £34 million in 2013–14, followed by annual maximum payments of £35 million from 2014–15 to 2032–33. The city council's share would largely come from the parking levy, which was expected to raise £9 million in 2012–13 and £10.3 million in 2013–14.

Phase 2 involved extensions to Chilwell and Beeston in the west and Clifton in the south. It would reuse the remaining piers of the old Great Central (GC) railway viaduct above Nottingham station, mostly

Two views of the Wilford Toll Bridge at different stages of construction.
**Left:** The north end of the bridge on 30 March 2013. In this view the former toll house, now used as a cafe, can be seen on the right.
**Right:** The south side of the bridge looking north on 19 May 2014. *Mike Haddon (3)*

**Above:** The present day tram route to Clifton South uses a short straight stretch of the former Great Central Main Line alignment through Wilford. British Railways Standard 9F 2-10-0 92083 hauls a southbound freight past Wilford on the GCML on 9 June 1965, just over a year before it closed as a through route (although an unconnected stub between Nottingham and Rugby remained open until 1969, and freight continued to use part of the line between Nottingham and East Leake until 1973). *Colourrail.com*

**Above:** Track laying in progress alongside the former Great Central Railway embankment on 15 April 2014, looking south-west towards Wilford Lane.

**Above:** The former Great Central Railway embankment has been cleared in readiness for the Phase 2 line to Clifton South taken on 25 May 2012, looking north from Ruddington Lane towards Compton Acres.

**Above:** Another view of the cleared former Great Central trackbed, taken on 6 March 2012 and looking south from Ruddington Lane towards the A52 road bridge. *Mike Haddon (3)*

dismantled in the 1980s. The final plan saw the Chilwell/Beeston route serve the Meadows area, Wilford/Ruddington Lane and the Clifton Estate, with a new Park & Ride site at the terminus serving the A453. The Chilwell/Beeston route would serve the Meadows residential area, the NG2 business park, Queens Medical Centre, University of Nottingham, the centre of Beeston and similarly a Park & Ride site at the terminus serving the A52, close to Junction 25 of the M1 motorway.

Construction of Phase 2 started with utility diversion work in November 2011. 30 January 2012 saw the start of the clearance of vegetation and trees from University Boulevard on the Toton Lane route and vegetation clearance on sections of the Clifton route. Later that year the first track was laid at Toton. By July that year preparatory work had started on the former Wilford Toll Bridge. On 11 February 2013 the first section of the bridge over Nottingham station was erected in the Taylor Woodrow Alstom yard south of the station, which was then moved into position over Queens Road in a series of overnight moves. By late March the second section of the bridge was under construction, and then the entire structure was moved into position over the station later in the year. Meanwhile on 24 February a 640 tonne span was installed across the Midland Main Line at Lenton South Junction. The first on-street track was laid on Meadows Way in April 2013.

Completion of Phase 2 had been scheduled for late 2014 but was around six months behind schedule because of construction delays, especially with diversion of water mains and power cables. Track laying was completed on 11 December 2014, and meanwhile the first powered test run on the Phase 2 network took place in the early hours of 22 August that year from Station Street via The Meadows to Wilford on the Clifton South line before returning to Station Street. Test running on the rest of the Phase 2 network began in early 2015. The first part of Phase 2 to open to passengers was the relocated Nottingham Station stop, which opened on 27 July 2015 and is located immediately to the south of its predecessor the original Station Street stop. This was followed by the opening of the rest of Phase 2, the lines to Toton Lane and Clifton South – both lines opened on 25 August 2015.

### OWNERSHIP CHANGES

As soon as funding had been secured for NET Phase 1, the scheme promoter Greater Nottingham Rapid Transit Ltd invited procurement tenders for the new system. Arrow Light Rail Ltd was set up as a

**Left:** Initial preparatory work for the new bridge carrying the Toton Lane line over the railway at Lenton South Junction has started as the 17.25 Leicester–Lincoln, formed of unit 158 812, passes this location on 25 May 2012.

**Below:** A year and a day later, on 26 May 2013, the bridge over Lenton South Junction has been lowered into position. This is the view looking east from Lenton Lane.

special purpose company to fund, design, build, operate and maintain the Phase 1 lines for a period of 30.5 years. Arrow Light Rail was a consortium consisting of six partners:

- Innisfree, an infrastructure investment group with experience in PFI schemes (30%)
- Galaxy Fund, a public transport infrastructure investor (20%)
- Nottingham City Transport, the city's publicly owned bus company (one of the UK's last remaining municipally owned operators, albeit with Transdev now holding an 18% stake in the company) (12.5%)
- Bombardier (originally ADtranz), the builder of the first batch of NET trams and historically a railway rolling stock manufacturer but by then also with a wider expertise in other aspects of railway and light rail operation (12.5%)
- Carillion Private Finance, part of the construction and facilities management company Carillion, which was formed in 1999 following a demerger from Tarmac (12.5%)
- Transdev, an international public transport management company based in France with experience of operating around 70 public transport systems (12.5%)

Arrow Light Rail continued to operate the system until 2011 when its operating contract was cancelled as part of the Government approval process for NET Phase 2. Arrow Light Rail did bid for the Phase 2 contract but lost out to a new consortium known as Tramlink Nottingham Ltd, comprising global investor and asset management company Meridiam (30%), OFI InfraVia (20%), Alstom Transport

**Above:** The bridge over the A52 Clifton Boulevard (which would be named the Ningbo Friendship Bridge two months after this photo was taken) is already in place as the ramp leading to it is under construction on Science Road on 10 March 2014. *Mike Haddon (3)*

**Right:** Future tramway route clearance is under way alongside Central College at Chilwell on 6 March 2012.

(12.5%), Keolis (12.5%), Vinci Investments (12.5%) and the Wellglade Group (12.5%). As with the Arrow Light Rail consortium, operation was further subcontracted to a consortium of Keolis (80%) and Wellglade (20%) with maintenance subcontracted to Alstom Transport. Because Wellglade owns bus company TrentBarton, which operates services across Nottinghamshire and Derbyshire, the new concession was referred to, and approved by, the Office of Fair Trading, with the finalised 23-year PFI contract being signed on 15 December 2011. Tramlink Nottingham then took over operations from Arrow Light Rail two days later.

A major advantage of the Arrow Light Rail concession was that because the consortium

**Left:** The bus station site in Styring Street, Beeston, is being redeveloped in preparation for the arrival of the tramway in this view, taken on 15 April 2014.

**Below:** The Toton Lane line under construction in Chilwell Road, Beeston, at the junction with Middle Street, also on 15 April 2014. *Mike Haddon (3)*

included bus operator Nottingham City Transport, NCT day tickets and Easyrider smartcards were also valid on the trams. Unfortunately the takeover by Tramlink Nottingham led to the loss of this facility with only the more expensive Kangaroo tickets (since superseded by the Robin Hood ticket range) remaining valid on both modes. On the other hand, from April 2014 until March 2020, thanks to Wellglade's ownership of bus operator TrentBarton, that operator's Mango smartcards could be used on NET. This

**Above:** Cator Lane stop nears completion on 22 April 2015, four months before the opening of the Phase 2 routes.

**Above:** 234 reverses on the crossover just north of Queens Walk, the first stop south of Nottingham Station on the Clifton South line, during "ghost running" on 14 March 2015. In the background can be seen the tower of St Mary's Church in the Lace Market, just north of Midland station. *Mike Haddon (2)*

**Above:** 235 stands at the Clifton South terminus with a service for Phoenix Park on the opening day of the two Phase 2 extensions, 25 August 2015. Note the red window sticker proclaiming "2500 new Park & Ride spaces now open".

arrangement ended with the introduction of new ticket machines on TrentBarton buses meaning that Mango cards were no longer compatible with NET ticket machines and validators (and in October 2020 Mango cards were withdrawn and replaced by a Mango app).

The Arrow Light Rail Concession that operated until 2011 also meant that, with NCT being part of the consortium, bus services were reorganised to fit in with the trams unlike in most other UK cities and conurbations with tramways or other forms of light rail system (such as Greater Manchester, Sheffield and Tyne & Wear) where bus deregulation had led buses to compete with tram and light rail services rather than

complementing them. In particular, services in the Bulwell area were revised with feeder buses connecting with the trams here.

Connecting you soon...

New lines, new trams!

Bringing Nottingham *together*    www.thetram.net

**Right:** A "New lines, new trams" poster at Wilford Village stop on 14 March 2014, just under a year and a half before the arrival of the tram service at this location. *Mike Haddon (2)*

**CHAPTER 3:**

# NOTTINGHAM EXPRESS TRANSIT
# ROUTE BY ROUTE

**Above:** Alstom Citadis tram 225 crosses the River Trent on Wilford Bridge – rebuilt for trams from the former toll bridge in 2014–15 – with an early morning service from Phoenix Park to Clifton South on 12 August 2021. *Robert Pritchard*

Nottingham Express Transit has two distinct north–south routes with a common core through the city centre, trams generally operating from Hucknall to Toton Lane (at 22.42 km the longer route) and Phoenix Park–Clifton South (15.52 km). For the first 11 years of operation, until August 2015, trams just operated on the main 12.3 km route from Station Street to Hucknall, plus from Station Street to Phoenix Park (for more detail on services see Chapter 6). Today, there are 50 stops on the system, including the four termini (this counts the separate platforms of Highbury Vale as one stop).

Whilst Phase 1 was able to take advantage of a number of current or former railway lines, by contrast on Phase 2 there was much less opportunity to reuse or share rail corridors and these lines saw a greater proportion of the route sharing road space with other traffic. The Phase 2 extensions also required the construction of five major structures to cross the Midland Main Line, River Trent and major highways. The greater element of street running did also mean the Phase 2 lines would be more integrated with existing urban settlements than Phase 1, although this led to greater impacts on communities during the construction phase. Phase 2 required the demolition of around 80 properties and the purchase of 500 plots of land – by contrast no properties were compulsorily purchased for Phase 1.

All measurements on NET are measured in kilometres (km). In terms of distances between stops, the majority of stops are located less than 1 km apart, but seven pairs of stops across the network are over 1 km apart. By far the furthest distance between stops at 1.61 km is Moor Bridge–Butler's Hill (on the northern section of the Hucknall line). The full list of those stops more than 1 km distant are:

| | |
|---|---|
| Moor Bridge–Butler's Hill | 1.61 km |
| Wilkinson Street–Basford | 1.24 km |

| | |
|---|---|
| Wilford Village–Wilford Lane | 1.20 km |
| Highbury Vale–Bulwell | 1.18 km |
| Ruddington Lane–Southchurch Drive North | 1.11 km |
| University of Nottingham–University Boulevard | 1.11 km |
| Nottingham Station–Meadows Way West | 1.04 km |

In terms of the stops that are closest together, there are ten pairs of stops that are less than 0.4 km apart. By no means all are in the city centre, and several are on the bi-directional single track sections in the Hyson Green area. The closest stops, at just 0.24 km apart, are The Forest and Noel Street – it takes not much more than a minute to walk between the two and both are visible from each other! The full list of stops less than 0.4 km apart are:

| | |
|---|---|
| The Forest–Noel Street | 0.24 km |
| Chilwell Road–High Road Central College | 0.26 km |
| Old Market Square–Royal Centre | 0.29 km |
| Beaconsfield Street–Shipstone Street | 0.31 km |
| Shipstone Street–Wilkinson Street | 0.32 km |
| Cator Lane–Bramcote Lane | 0.34 km |
| Noel Street–Beaconsfield Street | 0.35 km |
| Royal Centre–Nottingham Trent University | 0.37 km |
| Lace Market–Old Market Square | 0.37 km |
| Hyson Green Market–The Forest | 0.40 km |

All directions in the route guides below are given assuming that the reader is facing the direction of travel, and travelling away from Nottingham Station.

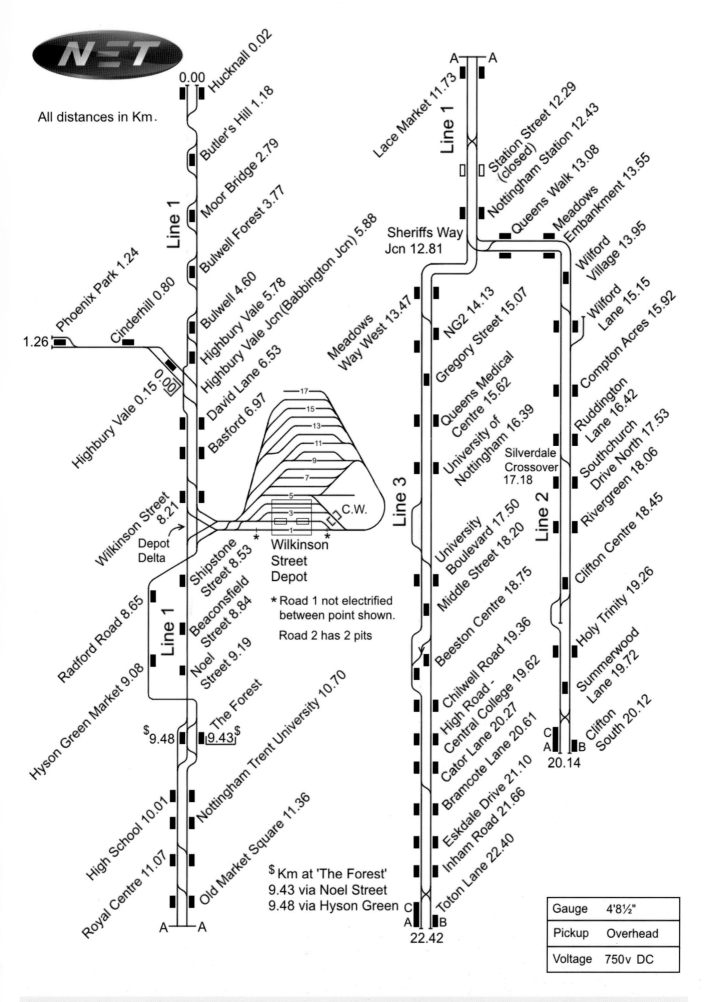

All distances in Km.

Hucknall 0.02

0.00

Butler's Hill 1.18

Moor Bridge 2.79

Bulwell Forest 3.77

Line 1

Phoenix Park 1.24

Cinderhill 0.80

1.26

Bulwell 4.60

Highbury Vale 5.78

Highbury Vale Jcn (Babbington Jcn) 5.88

David Lane 6.53

Highbury Vale 0.15

Basford 6.97

Wilkinson Street 8.21

Depot Delta

Shipstone Street 8.53

Beaconsfield Street 8.84

Noel Street 9.19

Radford Road 8.65

Line 1

Hyson Green Market 9.08

The Forest

Nottingham Trent University 10.70

$9.48

$9.43$

C.W.

*  Wilkinson Street Depot

17
15
13
11
9
7
5
3
1

* Road 1 not electrified between point shown.

Road 2 has 2 pits

High School 10.01

Royal Centre 11.07

Old Market Square 11.36

$ Km at 'The Forest'
9.43 via Noel Street
9.48 via Hyson Green

A — A

Lace Market 11.73

Line 1

A — A

Station Street 12.29 (closed)

Nottingham Station 12.43

Queens Walk 13.08

Meadows Embankment 13.55

Wilford Village 13.95

Wilford Lane 15.15

Compton Acres 15.92

Sheriffs Way Jcn 12.81

Meadows Way West 13.47

NG2 14.13

Gregory Street 15.07

Queens Medical Centre 15.62

University of Nottingham 16.39

Silverdale Crossover 17.18

Ruddington Lane 16.42

Southchurch Drive North 17.53

Rivergreen 18.06

Line 3

University Boulevard 17.50

Middle Street 18.20

Line 2

Clifton Centre 18.45

Beeston Centre 18.75

Chilwell Road 19.36

High Road - Central College 19.62

Cator Lane 20.27

Bramcote Lane 20.61

Eskdale Drive 21.10

Inham Road 21.66

Toton Lane 22.40

Holy Trinity 19.26

Summerwood Lane 19.72

Clifton South 20.12

C
A — B
20.14

C
A — B
22.42

| Gauge | 4'8½" |
|---|---|
| Pickup | Overhead |
| Voltage | 750v DC |

A line map showing the Nottingham Express Transit routes, kilometre distances between stops and the depot layout. *Martyn Brailsford/Branch Line Society*

**Above:** With its destination having already been changed to show Phoenix Park, 215 arrives at the original Nottingham Station stop, then called Station Street, to terminate on 22 October 2011. To the immediate right of the tram the scissors crossover can be seen and to the right the former High Pavement Chapel, now the "Pitcher & Piano" pub.

## PHASE 1: NOTTINGHAM STATION–HUCKNALL/ PHOENIX PARK

Visitors to Nottingham will most likely have their first encounter with NET in the city centre or at the Nottingham Station tram stop if arriving by train, although it is also possible to change onto the tram from Robin Hood Line trains at Hucknall or Bulwell. Anyone visiting the city by car may well find themselves driving on the roads used by the trams if arriving from the north, south or west, and may choose to park their car at one of the seven Park & Ride sites. As

Nottingham Station tram stop was the southern terminus of the NET system until the opening of Phase 2, and also where many visitors to the system will start their journey, it seems appropriate to start our tour here. Before the Phase 2 routes opened, the original tram stop (then known as Station Street) was located on a short remaining section of the former Great Central Railway viaduct immediately to the north of the present-day replacement stop and was linked by a footbridge across Station Street to the station footbridge. The second

**Below:** Spot the tram! A Bombardier Incentro tram can be seen crossing the former GCR viaduct as it approaches Nottingham Station stop on 30 June 2018. This view was taken from Nottingham Castle and the restored windmill at Green's Windmill & Science Centre at Sneinton can be seen in the distance. *Robert Pritchard (2)*

**Left:** 202 leaves the Lace Market stop and negotiates the sharpest curve on the system, as it turns from Fletcher Gate into Victoria Street, with a service for Hucknall on 25 October 2020. *Ian Beardsley*

Heading north first, the line passes over the Nottingham Canal almost immediately and there is then a scissors crossover. After this the site of the former Broadmarsh bus station and shopping centre is to the left and now being redeveloped. The former High Pavement Unitarian Chapel (now the Pitcher & Piano pub and restaurant, and Grade II listed) is to the right as the dedicated right of way over the tramway viaduct gives way to on-street running. A stop has been proposed to serve Broadmarsh for some years.

and current Nottingham Station stop is situated 0.14 km further south on a viaduct straddling Nottingham Midland station, which was named the Karlsruhe Friendship Bridge when it was officially opened on 17 October 2014, nine months before the new Nottingham Station tram stop opened. The naming acknowledged the technical support provided by Nottingham's twin city of Karlsruhe, Germany. The stop has direct access to the station both via the south concourse and via the station's main footbridge (although the latter route has no disabled access).

After climbing towards the city centre, firstly on Weekday Cross and then Fletcher Gate, the first intermediate city centre stop – surrounded by tall buildings such as shops and hotels – is Lace Market. This area of Nottingham was once the hub of the British Empire's lace industry. Nowadays the former red brick warehouses of this quarter-mile area have been regenerated as boutique shops, pubs or offices. It is also a protected heritage area.

Trams then slowly and carefully take a sharp left curve (the sharpest on the network) from Fletcher Gate onto Victoria Street,

**Above:** 207 has just left the Old Market Square stop and heads onto South Parade with an empty stock working on 17 July 2016. *Robert Pritchard*

**Above:** With the Council House illuminated, 227 pauses at Old Market Square with a service for Toton Lane on 4 September 2019.

## NOTTINGHAM EXPRESS TRANSIT FACT PANEL

| | |
|---|---|
| Population (City of Nottingham): | 337 100[1] (wider conurbation: 794 000[2]) |
| Route length: | 32 km (20 miles) |
| Number of stops: | 50 |
| Number of vehicles: | 37 (15 Bombardier Incentro AT6/5 and 22 Alstom Citadis 302) |

Sources:
[1] Office for National Statistics Mid-Year Population Estimates 2020
[2] United Nations World Population Prospects for 2021

which then becomes South Parade as we drop down to our next stop, Old Market Square. We pass the imposing Town Hall (or Council House as Nottingham City Council has always preferred to call it) on our right, with its 200 ft (61 m) high dome overlooking the square and a prominent feature for miles around. It was opened in 1929 and was designed by Nottingham architect TC Howitt.

Old Market Square is the busiest stop on the system and the focal point of Nottingham city centre. The square itself is

**Right:** Passing the landmark Council House, 221 gracefully curves round the Old Market Square to arrive at the stop of the same name bound for Station Street on 3 August 2014. This was almost a year before the Phase 2 extensions opened and the first of the new Citadis trams had just entered service on the existing Phase 1 routes.
*Robert Pritchard (2)*

**Left:** The Theatre Royal can be seen in the background as 208 descends Market Street on 3 August 2014 with a service for Station Street. *Robert Pritchard*

High School can be seen on the right, from which the next stop, High School, gets its name.

Leaving High School we bear left onto Mount Hooton Road. On our right we skirt around the edge of another of Nottingham's largest parks, the Forest Recreation Ground, part of which hosts the annual Nottingham Goose Fair. Then Noel Street joins from the left and we enter a segregated tram only section to drop down into the important The Forest tram stop. This is a busy three-track stop, with a large Park & Ride site (one of NET's original five P&R sites) on the right at the edge of the park. There are some interesting points of note with the track layout here, with two crossovers, a central reversing siding and platform that is not used during normal service but may be used during special events when trams turn back here (such as during the Goose Fair) and a short section of interlace track that is used by inbound trams using the centre platform.

After The Forest, the line crosses over the busy A6130 Gregory Boulevard, passing Hyson Green Community Centre to the left. After this the lines split and run as single lines in parallel roads as they pass through the narrower streets of the Hyson Green area. The southbound line trails in from Terrace Street on the left while the northbound single line crosses this line as it continues straight on via Noel Street, running along the left-hand side of the road which features some attractive Edwardian era houses. This long straight residential street has two tram stops, the first of which carries the same name as the street itself (and is just 0.24 km further on from The Forest) and the second, Beaconsfield Street, takes its name from a street that crosses Noel Street at that point at right angles. It had originally been planned to call this

a large paved public area with a vast array of shops and eating and drinking establishments on either side, and is a popular venue for markets, fairs etc. Sometimes a fair, such as the Christmas Market, may be in full swing, and a giant Ferris wheel can sometimes be seen (and ridden on) here. There are also a number of seating areas and fountains making this a very pleasant location to sit and watch the trams passing by. In just over an hour here you will be able to observe all trams in service on the network. The Grade II listed Queen's Chambers with its black and white gabled roof can be seen on the north side of the square.

After leaving the stop, the line curves to the right and climbs to skirt the edge of Old Market Square: there is a crossover here. We then take a gentle climb up Market Street towards the Theatre Royal, where we curve to the left and cross Upper Parliament Street as we arrive at the next stop, located adjacent to the theatre and appropriately named Royal Centre. There is another crossover immediately after this stop.

The line then continues in a north-westerly direction on Goldsmith Street, passing through the Nottingham Trent University campus – this was Nottingham's second university formed in 1992, having previously been part of the Trent Polytechnic. We now head gently downhill as we approach its namesake tram stop. Just before we arrive here, notable buildings adjacent to the tram tracks include Nottingham Business School on the right and then Nottingham Law School on the left. Just after departing this stop and now leaving the city centre behind, we are soon on tree-lined Waverley Street and run alongside the Nottingham General Cemetery on the left and the Arboretum, a historic 19th century park, on the right. Just after the Arboretum ends, the buildings of Nottingham

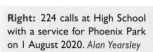

**Right:** 224 calls at High School with a service for Phoenix Park on 1 August 2020. *Alan Yearsley*

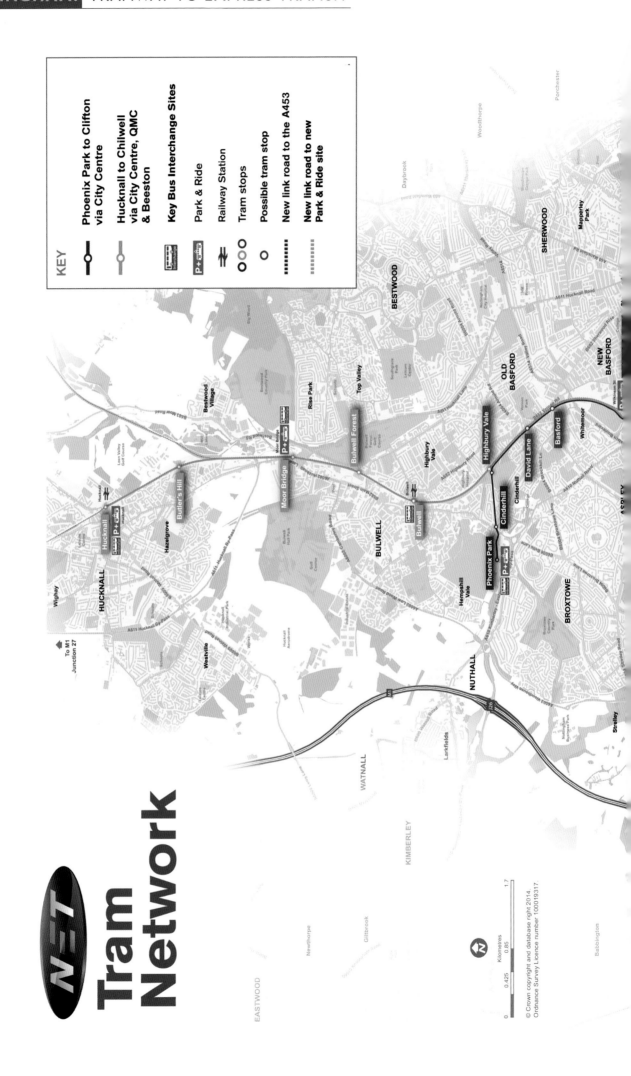

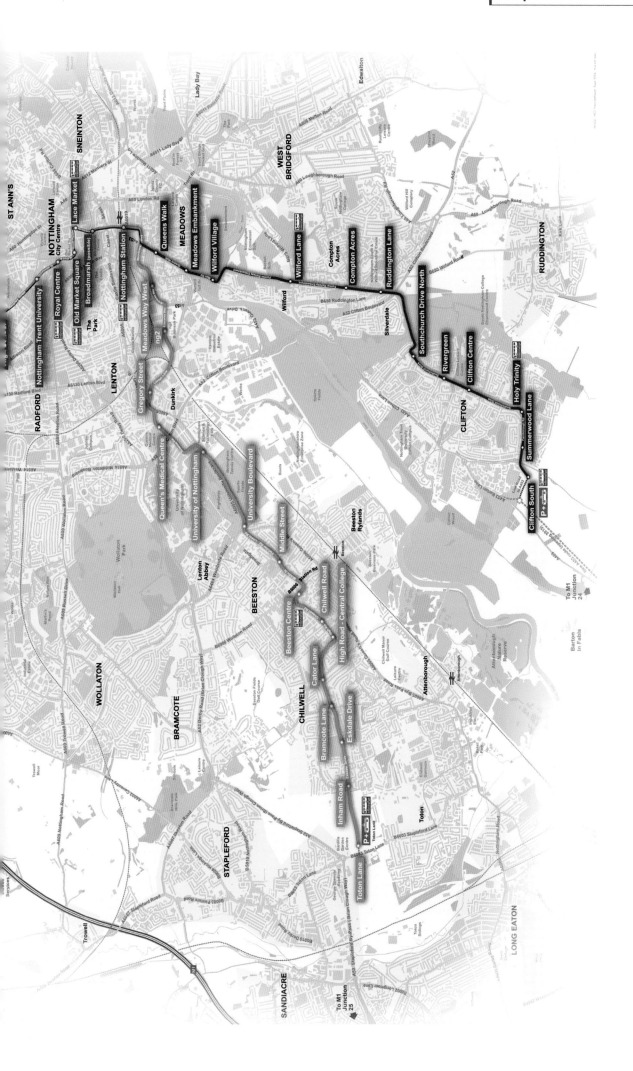

**Above:** 221 climbs Mount Hooton Road, between The Forest and High School stops, passing one of the entrances to the Forest Recreation Ground on 3 August 2014.

**Above:** With the red brick Hyson Green Community Centre behind, 218 leaves The Forest for Hucknall on 3 August 2014. Note the short section of interlace track in the foreground. *Robert Pritchard (2)*

**Above:** The layout of The Forest stop is illustrated, with 229 leaving with a Toton Lane service and the island platform and section of interlace track and crossover visible in this 1 August 2020 view. *Alan Yearsley*

stop Berridge Road and it would have been located slightly further south. Both single platform kerbside style stops are on the west side of the line and all three of these stations (The Forest, Noel Street and Beaconsfield Street) are visible from each other. The two single lines have run parallel until this point, and glimpsing left out of a tram as you pass side streets you may catch sight of a city-bound tram heading south on the other line. After the Beaconsfield Street stop we leave Noel Street and take a sharp left turn to drop down onto Gladstone Street, with St Mary's Catholic Primary School to the right. From here the line swings diagonally to the right onto Shipstone Street, which is also the name of the last stop on the northbound-only section, adjacent to Shipstone Street play area and just a stone's throw from the main administrative hub of NET and the depot.

The line then crosses Radford Road at a busy road

and tram interchange and joins the southbound line on Wilkinson Street. Just before Wilkinson Street tram stop the depot access lines branch off to the right, and this is immediately followed by another Park & Ride site adjacent to the stop. There are double-track connections to the depot from both the north and south side as part of the junction known as the Depot Delta; this junction, and the line beyond Wilkinson Street, is located on segregated track.

**Right:** 227 accelerates away from the camera from Noel Street as it heads along the street of the same name en-route to Phoenix Park on 10 October 2021. *Robert Pritchard*

**Left:** The Forest, Noel Street and Beaconsfield Street stops are all relatively close together and can be seen from each other. On 12 September 2021 203 arrives at the latter stop with a Hucknall service.

**Right:** One of the tightest fits in terms of stops is Shipstone Street, shoehorned between the narrow road of the same name and the play area to the right. On 12 September 2021 227 arrives with a service for Hucknall. It is also worth noting that some trams, mainly in the late evening, terminate here before heading empty to the depot. With just the display "Shipstone Street" on the blinds this can lead to confusion on the south side of the city to unwary passengers who have never heard of this somewhat obscure street and wonder if the tram is indeed heading into the city centre at all!

**Above:** Heading along the route of one of the old Nottingham Corporation tramways, 221 approaches the Radford Road stop with a service for Toton Lane on 10 October 2021. *Robert Pritchard (3)*

**Left:** Having just left the Shipstone Street stop, 233 drops down towards the Wilkinson Street stop with a Hucknall service on 10 October 2021. The line to the right is the inbound single line which heads for Radford Road. The building to the left is the landmark Shipstones Business Centre, rebuilt from the 1900-built Shipstones Brewery, which closed in 1991. *Robert Pritchard*

**Below:** Part of the complex track layout at Wilkinson Street is illustrated as 232 heads away from the camera and is about to turn right onto Radford Road and onto the city-bound one-way section on 1 August 2020. *Alan Yearsley*

Heading back briefly towards the city centre, southbound trams follow the same route from the Wilkinson Street stop for the short distance as far as the end of Wilkinson Street but then turn right onto Radford Road instead of continuing straight on, likewise running along the left-hand side of the road. This follows a section of the original Nottingham Corporation Bulwell Market tram route.

There are two intermediate stops on this section served only by city-bound trams: Radford Road stop is surrounded by small independent shops on the left-hand side of its namesake street and housing estates on the right, and Hyson Green Market stop is located on a short reserved section of track adjacent to a large Asda supermarket. With Nottingham Law Centre on the right, the line then curves sharply to the left onto Terrace Street where it runs around the side of the Asda store, with Hyson Green Youth Club to the right. At the junction with Noel Street we cross over and then run alongside the northbound line back to The Forest stop and then trams continue towards the city centre.

Continuing back to the Wilkinson Street stop to head north, the stop lies adjacent to the depot and control centre (see Chapter 5) and driver changes will sometimes take place here. Immediately after the Wilkinson Street stop the line crosses over, and then sweeps round a tight curve to run alongside the Robin Hood railway line, leaving behind the reserved track section and running on its own dedicated right of way for the rest of the journey to Phoenix Park or Hucknall. The tram picks up speed on the longer run between stops here, and to the right several trams can sometimes be seen stabled in the depot sidings. From here the tramway is mainly on

**Above:** 221 leaves the David Lane stop for the city centre and Toton Lane on 10 October 2021. *Robert Pritchard*

**Left:** 234 runs alongside the River Leen and popular adjacent footpath between David Lane and Highbury Vale as it heads north for Phoenix Park on 10 October 2021.

**Right:** Showing the junction at Highbury Vale, 213 heads for Hucknall as the lines to the Phoenix Park branch stop at Highbury Vale head to the right, in this 26 August 2013 view.

**Left:** Phoenix Park branch trams will often pass at Highbury Vale. On 10 October 2021 217 on the left is working a Phoenix Park–Clifton South service and 206 on the right a Clifton South–Phoenix Park service. *Robert Pritchard (3)*

**Left:** On the Phoenix Park branch, 206 crosses the River Leen on the edge of Mill Street Recreation Ground as it arrives at the Highbury Vale stop on 10 October 2021.

Lincoln Street Water Meadows to the left. Parts of the River Leen had to be realigned along here to accommodate the new double track tramway. One of the original Nottingham Corporation lines, to Bulwell Market, ran along the parallel Vernon Road, to the right of the railway line.

Crossing David Lane we arrive immediately at the stop of the same name, the last stop at which both Hucknall and Phoenix Park trams call at the same platforms. The level crossing here is equipped with full barriers for the railway and traffic lights for the tramway. From David Lane a footpath parallels the line and the River Leen, giving good views of the trams and Robin Hood Line trains. The River Leen, which originates on high ground above Newstead Abbey, has long been regarded as one of the country's cleaner rivers, and although for much its length it runs through the heart of the city it is a great place to spot wildlife such as kingfishers and heron.

The next stop, Highbury Vale, has separate island platforms for the

**Below:** Rarely photographed Cinderhill, the only stop on the 1.26 km Phoenix Park branch, gives the impression of being a wayside country halt. On 12 September 2021 206 arrives with a Phoenix Park–Clifton South service. There is almost always a tram in section on the branch, note the dot-matrix destination shows the next Phoenix Park tram in two minutes – this tram will pass this service at the Highbury Vale stop. *Robert Pritchard (2)*

ballasted track, with concrete sleepers. The overhead line equipment also changes to catenary suspension, allowing wider pole spacing.

As the tramway heads away from Wilkinson Street we cross the River Leen and the River Leen Greenway runs alongside us on our left until the line passes under the A6514 Western Boulevard, and shortly afterwards we arrive at the next stop, Basford. A footbridge gives access across the railway lines. The line then continues in a north-westerly direction alongside the double track Robin Hood Line on the right and the River Leen on the left – initially alongside

Hucknall and Phoenix Park lines, with the Phoenix Park line curving off to the left just before we arrive at the Hucknall line platform. There is also a crossover just before the junction. The River Leen also curves away to the left and runs alongside the Phoenix Park line platform, then passes underneath the Phoenix Park branch and swings towards the Hucknall line once again. To the left of the Phoenix Park line platform lies the large Mill Street Recreation Ground.

### The Phoenix Park line

The Phoenix Park line is a short 1.26 km single track branch with just one intermediate stop at Cinderhill. It runs over part of the course of a former Midland Railway Cinderhill Colliery Railway mineral line that once served Babbington Colliery (also known locally as Cinderhill Colliery). The mine opened in 1842 to serve what was the first large-scale coal mine in Nottinghamshire. The mine had a long life, closing in January 1986, after which the site was redeveloped into the Phoenix Business Park. The railway line serving the colliery, which was also single track, opened in 1877 and closed in 1983.

**Above:** The Phoenix Park terminus is located on the former colliery site, now regenerated as part of a Business Park and Park & Ride car park. On 1 August 2020 202 stands at the terminus. *Alan Yearsley*

The one intermediate stop on today's tram line, Cinderhill, is located in a shallow cutting halfway between the Bagnall Road and Cinderhill Road underbridges, which are both original brick railway bridges dating from the 1870s. Cinderhill, one of the quieter stops on the system, is also the only stop on the entire NET system where trams use the same platform in both directions. After climbing underneath Cinderhill Road, the line crosses over and then runs alongside Millennium Way East on segregated track as it passes through the Phoenix Business Park complex for the rest of the journey up to the Phoenix Park terminus. A two-track island platform stop at what is the smallest terminus on the network serves a modest Park & Ride site, but there is very little residential development nearby. Trams normally use the left-hand platform here.

### The Hucknall line

Continuing along the Hucknall line from Highbury Vale, it is 1.18 km to the next stop at Bulwell. We curve gently to the right to head north and the River Leen is now once again in close proximity on the left and runs almost immediately next to the line for a short stretch just before we arrive at Bulwell. This is the only intermediate stop to be served by both trams and Robin Hood Line trains. Immediately before the stop Bulwell Riverside Library is situated to the left and there is also a crossover. The original Bulwell station opened at the same time as the Midland Railway's Nottingham–Mansfield line on 2 October 1848 but closed to passengers along with all other stations on the line in 1964. In 1993 the Robin Hood Line reopened to passengers as far as Newstead, with Bulwell station reopening on 23 May 1994. Bulwell is a market town of around 30 000 population.

Until the arrival of the tramway in 2004, Bulwell was a two-platform station with a northbound and a southbound platform; however, to make way for the tramway the section between Bulwell and Hucknall was singled and the northbound platform demolished, since when trains in both directions have used the erstwhile southbound platform. The tram stop consists of an island platform alongside the heavy rail line, and the station car park is located to the left of the tram stop. Unfortunately when the tramway opened the opportunity was not taken to provide easy step-free access between the tram stop and the Robin Hood Line station, and the original non-Disability Discrimination Act-compliant footbridge was retained, albeit giving access between the station and the tram stop instead

**Above:** Passing under one of the old brick railway bridges either side of the Cinderhill stop on 12 September 2021, 206 prepares to climb towards the Phoenix Park terminus – at first on this slab track section and then alongside a road. Note how the OLE poles match the tram livery. *Robert Pritchard*

**Left:** Amid some glorious autumn colours, 213 leaves Bulwell for Toton Lane on 10 October 2021. *Robert Pritchard*

**Below:** In NET promotional livery, 209 leaves Bulwell Forest with a service for Station Street on 8 July 2014. *Mike Haddon*

**Below:** At Moor Bridge on 12 September 2021, 220 is just leaving for Hucknall as 214 heads for Toton Lane. The Robin Hood Line is to the right. *Robert Pritchard*

of between the southbound and the now demolished northbound platform. Because of this, any passengers who wish to change between tram and train here must cross over the northbound tram track and then via the footbridge onto the station platform. The station does have step-free access off Station Road, but it would be unadvisable for a person with disabilities to attempt to change between the two modes here as they would have to take a rather long and convoluted route! It remains to be seen whether this matter will be rectified at some point in the future.

Limited clearances north of Bulwell mean that the tramway is also forced to make do with just one single track alongside the heavy rail line as it heads in a north-easterly direction to the next stop, Bulwell Forest. Like all three intermediate stops between Bulwell and Hucknall this is an island platform with a loop. Bulwell Forest and Butler's Hill are the normal crossing points during the 7.5 minute peak services, whilst during the 10 or 15 minute off-peak/evening or Sunday service, Moor Bridge is the normal crossing point. Just before the Bulwell Forest stop St Alban's Road crosses, with a CCTV full barrier controlled crossing operated remotely by Network Rail. A large retail unit housing Wickes, Poundland and Matalan, amongst others, lies to the left of the stop and just to the north is a large Morrisons store. The tramway becomes single track once again but the heavy rail line becomes a double track loop known as the Bestwood Park Loop, which continues as far as the next stop, Moor Bridge. Between Bulwell Forest and Moor Bridge stops we pass Bulwell Forest golf course on the right, and just before Moor Bridge stop the River Leen passes beneath the line from left to right once again and is on our right for the rest of the journey.

Moor Bridge includes the smallest Park & Ride on the system, with 119 spaces, and this stop also serves the Bulwell Hall estate, which lies to the west. Bayles & Wylies foot crossing, just north of the stop, was replaced by a large disability compliant footbridge in 2013 following the tragic death of a 13-year-old girl on the foot

crossing in 2012. Heading north, the area through which we pass becomes less built-up as housing estates give way to parkland and open countryside at least on the right-hand side, where the line passes Mill Lakes. Beyond it is the much larger Bestwood Country Park, part of which is on a reclaimed colliery site. Meanwhile, more modern housing developments line the route to the west side of the line. Trams regularly reach their maximum speed of 70 km/h on the northern end of the Hucknall line, and at 1.61 km Moor Bridge to Butler's Hill is by some distance the longest gap between stops on the system.

The River Leen swings away to the right as we approach the last intermediate stop, Butler's Hill. From here Brickyard Drive crosses the line on a CCTV controlled half-barrier level crossing as we head in a north-westerly direction and pass residential neighbourhoods on the left and industrial units on the right, soon arriving at the terminus of Hucknall. Just before the terminus large Argos and Tesco Extra stores can be seen on the left. Hucknall is another market town in the Ashfield district of Nottinghamshire with a population of around 32 000. It lies about seven miles (11.25 km) north of Nottingham. There is a bus, tram and rail interchange with two tram platforms here, the right-hand platform being one side of an island platform shared with the single-track heavy rail station, trains continuing north to Mansfield and Worksop. This gives step-free access between the tramway and the Robin Hood Line and is thus a much more convenient location for interchange between the two modes than at Bulwell. Trams use both platforms here regularly as one will normally arrive just before another returns south, so there is plenty of opportunity for getting photos of two trams together. Unlike the Phase 2 extension termini, the platforms are not given letters, and the platforms themselves are also shorter, only being able to accommodate one tram in each. A Park & Ride site with space for more than 400 cars lies to the west of the terminus.

Around 4 km of Phase 1 features on-street running, less than 30%. This is less than both of the southern branches of Phase 2.

**Below:** A general view of the Hucknall terminus on 28 August 2013. 203 is in the tram terminus platforms, with the single railway platform to the left. *Robert Pritchard*

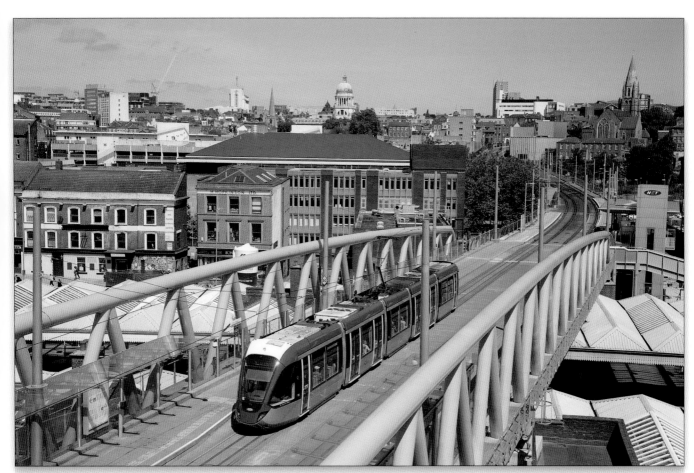

**Above:** The top level of the Nottingham Station multi-storey car park gives a great view of trams crossing the Karlsruhe Friendship Bridge, with the city centre as a backdrop. On 17 July 2016 229 heads towards the city with a Hucknall service. Visible to the right of the tram are the former platforms of Station Street stop before it was moved further south in 2015.

## PHASE 2: NOTTINGHAM STATION–TOTON LANE/CLIFTON SOUTH

### The Toton Lane line

We return to Nottingham Station for our tour of the Phase 2 routes, which fully opened to passengers on 25 August 2015, as covered in Chapter 2. Just after leaving the station, the line heads south downhill on a ramp from the old railway viaduct and then swings to the right across Arkwright Street onto Meadows Way. At this point the dedicated right of way ends and the line runs on-street, continuing along Meadows Way past the junction (officially called Sheriffs Way Junction) with the Clifton South line.

For Toton Lane trams this is one of the longest distances between stops, but Meadows Way soon curves to the left and then to the right as it heads towards the first stop, Meadows Way West.

The A453 Queens Drive then swings in from the right and runs alongside Meadows Way, with industrial estates and retail units dominating the landscape on the right and housing estates on the left. Meadows Way, on which the tramway runs, then curves to the left once again and heads due south. As it does so the tram tracks curve off to

the right (passing Meadows Police Station on the left) onto Enterprise Way and there is a crossover as we head due west as far as the next stop – NG2 being one of the more unusual (and shortest!) tram stop names in the UK. The stop serves the NG2 Business Park which was developed in the early 2000s and is named after the postal district where it is located. NG2 is now home to some of the city's biggest employers and includes various new car showrooms, one of the

**Right:** 229 runs off the former GCR railway viaduct, having just left the Nottingham Station stop, with a service for Toton Lane on 9 April 2019. *Robert Pritchard (2)*

**Left:** This is Sheriffs Way Junction, where the Clifton South and Toton Lane lines diverge on a street running section not far from Nottingham Station. On 25 August 2015, opening day for the Phase 2 lines, 227 negotiates the junction with a Clifton South–Phoenix Park service. *Paul Abell*

**Below:** 228 leaves the NG2 stop with a service for Toton Lane on 20 April 2016. *Mike Haddon*

Specsavers head offices and various solicitors and the like. Given the lack of nearby housing NG2 can be one of the least used tram stops on the network at certain times of day and at weekends, however.

As the line reaches the far end of Enterprise Way and the NG2 complex it climbs onto a flyover and runs through the edge of King's Meadow Nature Reserve, then crosses over the Midland Main Line between Nottingham and Beeston stations on a new bridge. As it does so the triangle junction for the Erewash Valley route to Chesterfield via Trowell

**Left:** 216 leaves the NG2 Business Park as it is about to exit the street running section to cross the Midland Main Line with a service for Toton Lane on 17 July 2016. *Robert Pritchard*

facilities including its namesake, Nottingham NHS Treatment Centre, Nottingham Children's Hospital, Nottingham University Hospital, and the University of Nottingham Medical School – said to be the second largest hospital complex in the UK. NET says that the Queens Medical Centre is also the only hospital in the UK with a direct link to a tram network, with the stop conveniently located between the South Block and Treatment Centre (lifts and stairs connect the stop to the different hospital complexes). A bus stop close by also connects the "Medilink" bus service to other parts of the hospital site and the City Hospital. It is also worth noting that there are special power feed arrangements here, to prevent stray currents interfering with sensitive hospital equipment and to reduce noise and vibrations from the trams.

Junction can be seen on the right. The tramway then heads in a north-westerly direction along Lenton Lane and through a small industrial park to the next stop, Gregory Street. Just before this stop it crosses the Beeston Canal. Gregory Street has one of the few island platforms on a normal double track section of NET.

Shortly after leaving Gregory Street and now in the Dunkirk district of the city, the line takes a sharp left turn. Following a short section of running on side reservation alongside Abbey Street (the A6005) the tramway then leaves street running behind as it rises onto an elevated section to cross the River Leen and then arrives at the Queens Medical Centre stop. This is located within a vast complex of medical

Immediately after the stop, the line crosses one of the hospital car parks and the A52 Clifton Boulevard on an impressive bow string bridge (with footpath alongside) named the Ningbo Friendship Bridge – the largest structure on the tram network. The bridge's naming was performed on 11 June 2014 by the Vice-Mayor of Ningbo, China, to acknowledge the links between the city of Ningbo and the University of Nottingham. Once it has crossed over the A52, our tram

**Left:** 237 calls at Queens Medical Centre with a service for Hucknall on the opening day of the Phase 2 extensions, 25 August 2015. *Mike Haddon*

**Below:** 221 crosses the bow string bridge on the approach to the Queens Medical Centre stop with a service for Hucknall on 10 October 2021. *Ian Beardsley*

takes a rather curvaceous route through the University of Nottingham campus whose buildings predate the tramway by several decades meaning that the tram route had to be planned around the structures already in place instead of the other way round (as with certain other light rail projects such as the Manchester Metrolink Eccles extension).

After passing the Nottingham Lakeside Arts Centre, the University of Nottingham Museum and Djanogly Art Gallery the line takes a sharp curve to the right before reaching University of Nottingham tram stop, located adjacent to Highfields Park Adventure Golf Course and Highfields Boating Lake and

**Left:** 204 leaves the busy University of Nottingham stop with a service for Toton Lane on 20 April 2016. *Mike Haddon*

There is also a crossover here. Opposite and to the left are a number of sports complexes – including Nottingham Tennis Centre, Beeston Hockey Club, Highfields Sports Complex and Nottingham Lacrosse Club.

After the University Boulevard stop the line reverts to on-street running as we enter the Broxtowe borough and run in a south-westerly direction along Lower Road, which later becomes Fletcher Road and then the B6464 Middle Street from which the next stop gets its name. A notable feature of Middle Street, particularly from its namesake tram stop southwards, is that as the road widens the northbound and southbound tram track run at or close to the edge of the

serving the main campus of the University. Shortly after leaving this stop the Trent Building, with its famous clock tower, can be seen in the distance on the other side of the boating lake. The line now crosses the University Boulevard and runs on a segregated alignment to the south side of the road, the longer section between stops here allowing for some brief faster running. The University's main buildings, dating from 1922, can be seen to the right. Just before the University Boulevard stop (serving the edge of the campus) there is a loop line or storage siding that can be used by city-bound trams or to recess a tram if needed.

road rather than side by side. Middle Street stop, located just after the line crosses Humber Road, is an island platform. For a short stretch of Middle Street near Beeston town centre, the road is so wide that the city-bound track has another lane of traffic and a cycle lane between it and the pavement.

As the line passes a large Tesco store to the right, it takes a sharp right turn onto Styring Street before reaching the busy Beeston Centre tram stop, which forms part of a bus and tram interchange located adjacent to the town's main retail quarter. The tracks widen and with

**Left:** On the ballasted track between University of Nottingham and University Boulevard, 225 heads for Toton Lane on 12 August 2021. To the left is the refuge loop for inbound trams, the only such loop on the system.

**Below:** University Boulevard is a busy stop for students. On the morning of 23 September 2019 217 arrives with a service for Hucknall. *Robert Pritchard (2)*

two staggered island platforms, trams use the two outer sides of the bus and tram shelters and the connecting bus services the inner sides. This area was extensively redeveloped in the early 2010s to accommodate the tramway. There is a crossover just before the stop.

On departure from Beeston Centre, and with the town centre itself to the right, we take another sharp curve around the impressive St John's Church, Beeston, which can be seen on the left,

**Left:** Beeston Centre offers interchange with a number of local bus routes. On 31 July 2015, just a few weeks before the line opened to passengers, 225 stands with a test run to Nottingham Station. *Mike Haddon*

College (this is just 0.26 km from Chilwell Road, the second closest pair of stops on the network). This stop gets its name from the college of further and higher education located adjacent to the city-bound platform of the tram stop, although at the time of writing this is not currently used by students following a merger of educational establishments – but may be redeveloped as student accommodation.

then head once more in a south-westerly direction along Chilwell Road, the continuation of the B6464 road, as far as its namesake tram stop (also passing the spire of Beeston Methodist Church to the left). A number of independent businesses, eating establishments and hairdressers line this road. Chilwell Road then becomes High Road, and shortly afterwards the tramway parts company with the road onto a dedicated right of way at the next stop, High Road – Central

Now in the Chilwell district the line now takes a sharp right turn and heads in a north-westerly direction on ballast track and runs with high fences either side separating it from residential developments. Passing a substation on the right, it then crosses Cator Lane, after which the next stop is named. There is then only a short distance to the following stop, Bramcote Lane, running alongside a footpath down a tree-lined avenue. There is a crossover just before the stop. After

**Left:** Passing St John's Church as it heads down Middle Street in Beeston, 223 forms a Hucknall–Toton Lane service on 17 July 2016.

**Below:** The second church slightly further along Middle Street, Beeston Methodist Church, is seen here as 209 passes with a service for Toton Lane on 17 July 2016. *Robert Pritchard (2)*

the Bramcote Lane stop the line crosses over the road by this name.

The next two stops – the last two intermediate stops before the terminus – are also named after roads with which the line interfaces: Eskdale Drive runs alongside the line from just before its namesake stop as far as the following stop, Inham Road, after which the line crosses the road of that name. At Eskdale Drive the Inham Nook Recreation Ground lies on the right-hand side of the line. To the left are two schools – Alderman Pounder Infant School & Nursery is immediately adjacent to the stop whilst Eskdale Junior School lies slightly further on.

After Inham Road, the last intermediate stop, we leave the built-up residential area behind and pass through open countryside on both sides of the line until we reach the terminus at Toton Lane. A rural footpath crosses the line just before the terminus. Toton Lane is located on the northern edge of the small village of Toton and has an extensive Park & Ride site with over 1400 spaces. The site is located adjacent to the A52 Stapleford bypass, just one mile (1.6 km) east of Junction 25 of the M1 motorway, and is also convenient for a number of other nearby settlements such as Chilwell, Stapleford, and Sandiacre.

There is a scissors crossover just before the terminus and the two platforms can accommodate two trams each. The north platform is numbered "A" and "C" and the south side platform is numbered "B" nearest the buffer stops and can also accommodate a second tram but there is not a platform edge each. The north platform is numbered "A" and "C" and the south side platform is numbered "B" nearest the buffer stops and can

**Left:** 231 heads away from the camera, passing the crossover between Bramcote Lane and Cator Lane with a service for Hucknall on 12 August 2021. *Robert Pritchard*

**Below:** The most rural stretch on the whole system is immediately after departure from Toton Lane, with a short section of open countryside on both sides. On 10 October 2021 229 heads towards its first stop at Inham Road with a service for Hucknall. *Ian Beardsley*

also accommodate a second tram but there is not a platform edge at the country end. The stop includes a small shop which is usually open until lunchtime. From Sheriffs Way Junction (where the Toton Lane and Clifton South lines diverge) to the terminus the Toton Lane branch is 9.61 km, around half of which is on segregated track.

Toton is of course a name well known within railway enthusiast circles and those with a railway interest may like to take a

**Below:** On 30 June 2018 227 arrives at the Toton Lane terminus (it is about to cross over) with a service from Hucknall. *Robert Pritchard*

**Right:** On 30 June 2018 211 departs from the usually used Platform "A" at Toton Lane with a service for Hucknall. *Robert Pritchard*

footpath that leaves the main road almost opposite the Toton Lane terminus and proceeds across fields for just short of a mile to Toton bank – a location popular for railway enthusiasts for decades, overlooking DB Cargo's Toton depot. This is the largest locomotive depot in the country and there is always much of interest to see from Toton bank and it makes a pleasant location to spend an hour or so on a fine day, with the Erewash Valley freight line visible in the foreground as well. Previously the depot was operated

**Left:** Toton Lane terminus can hold four trams, with three platformed. Unusually it did hold three trams on the afternoon of 14 October 2016. Not in service cars 211 and 232 are seen in Platforms B and A respectively, with 221 forming a service to Hucknall in Platform C. *Ian Beardsley*

by English, Welsh & Scottish Railway (EWS) (and before that British Rail) and one of your co-authors remembers visiting an excellent open day held on site in 1998 – future large open days seem unlikely today, unfortunately!

The exterior of the Toton Lane stop, which lies in the middle of the large Park & Ride site, seen on 12 August 2021. *Robert Pritchard*

**Above:** With Queens Walk Community Centre to the right, 205 leaves the Queens Walk stop with a service for Clifton South on 9 April 2019.

### The Clifton South line

To take the Clifton South line, which is just over 2 km shorter than the Toton Lane line, we retrace our journey as far as the junction of Meadows Way and Sheriffs Way, where we now take a sharp left turn onto a segregated right of way. The initial section of the former Great Central Railway route from Nottingham has been lost and the tramway had to take a new alignment out of the city. The line initially heads in a south-westerly direction down the attractive tree-lined Queens Walk (confined to trams, bikes and pedestrians), with Queens Drive Recreation Ground on the right and the Queens Walk footpath on the left, from which the first intermediate stop gets its name. Queens Walk stop is adjacent to the local community centre. We then cross over Robin Hood Way, and Queens Walk still runs alongside us on our left as far as the next stop, Meadows Embankment.

We then pass the edge of Victoria Embankment, a park stretching along the north bank of the River Trent as far as the nearby Wilford Suspension Bridge, located out of sight around the curvaceous River to the left. The tramway itself passes the iconic red-brick Old Toll Booth on the left, now in use as the "Bridge Sandwich Bar", then crosses the Trent by means of the Wilford Toll Bridge, one of the most impressive structures on the whole tramway. This bridge opened as a private toll bridge in 1870 and was acquired by Nottingham City Council in 1969 but closed to road traffic in 1974 because of its poor condition. It reopened as a pedestrian and

cycle bridge in 1980 and was rebuilt and widened to accommodate the double-track tram line in 2014–15, still with a footpath/cycleway alongside. To the left of the bridge the imposing statue of Sir Robert Juckes Clifton can be seen on Victoria Embankment. Sir Robert was MP from 1861 until his death from typhoid in 1869 and funded a church, school and the Wilford Toll Bridge. When he died around 20 000 people attended his funeral. The statue was built around 1870.

Once on the south side of the River Trent, the line passes Nottingham Moderns Rugby Football Club on the right and Willow Meadows wildlife area on the left as it reaches the next stop, Wilford Village, an island platform. This area was poorly served by public transport

**Right:** 233 crosses the Wilford Bridge with a service for Clifton South on 9 April 2019. As seen from this angle, the footpath runs alongside the left-hand side of the bridge. *Robert Pritchard (2)*

**Right:** The Wilford Village stop is an island platform, with Nottingham Moderns Rugby Football Club to the right. 228 leaves with a Phoenix Park service on 12 August 2021.

before the opening of the tramway. The line then takes a sharp left turn, paralleling Corporation Avenue, followed by a sharp right turn, after which we are running alongside and then on the former Great Central Railway alignment, initially on ballasted track with a wide footpath and cycleway alongside providing good views of trams. There are two foot crossings on this section, the longer distance (just over 1 km) between Wilford Village and Wilford Lane and the straighter nature of the route allows for a brief section of 70 km/h running. As we scoot along, Wilford village is on our right and on our left we pass two secondary schools, the Nottingham Emmanuel School and the Beckett School whose grounds are separated by the Gresham Playing Fields and Gresham Sports Park. Just after the Beckett School we arrive at the other stop that takes its name from the village of Wilford, Wilford Lane, serving the Compton Acres district and the West Bridgford district to our left. There is a crossover just before the stop and a refuge siding and a fenced-in small maintenance compound/substation alongside the outbound platform.

After Wilford Lane we cross over the busy road after which the stop is named and are once again surrounded by housing estates on both sides. We are now on the route of the former GC Main Line (still with the footpath to the left, with a fence separating it and the tramway) to the next stop. The very straight stretch again allows for some higher speeds than on much of the rest of the network. Ruddington Lane Recreation Ground is to the right just before the Compton Acres stop, accessed by a footpath from both sides. There is a much shorter distance to the next stop, Ruddington Lane. Nottingham South & Wilford Industrial Estate is to the left before the stop (formerly brickworks were on this site), which is the last on the former GC alignment.

After crossing over the street named after the latter stop we then immediately pass under the A52 Clifton Boulevard dual-carriageway as we swing right and leave the former GCR alignment. It is again more than 1 km to the next stop and now with open countryside to the

left the route suddenly feels more rural. Part of the open land makes up Wilwell Farm Nature Reserve. Around halfway to the next stop there is another crossover – the Silverdale Crossover. The footpath and cycleway again parallels the line, this time to our right, and there are also a couple of foot crossings.

Just after the crossover, the line crosses over the Fairham Brook on a new bridge and then changes to on-street running as it curves onto Farnborough Road just before the busy junction with Southchurch Drive. We then take a sharp left to our next stop, Southchurch Drive North. The line now heads in a south-westerly direction as a traditional street tramway through the large residential area of Clifton, with a single high-rise tower block to our right. There are two further intermediate stops along Southchurch Drive at Rivergreen (alongside Clifton Methodist Church) and Clifton Centre. Rivergreen serves Nottingham Trent University's Clifton Campus.

The latter stop is located in Clifton's main shopping area, as the name suggests – with a number of shops to the right. Clifton Leisure Centre is to the left just before the stop and the large Clifton Medical Practice is opposite the stop. Clifton Centre has an island platform and is a busy stop. There is also a centre reversing siding that can be used

**Below:** Citadis tram 225 climbs onto the Wilford Bridge with a service for Clifton South on 12 August 2021. Seen on the right is the old toll booth office, whilst to the left of that – and alongside his famous bridge – is the statue of Sir Robert Juckes Clifton. *Robert Pritchard (2)*

**Right:** 225 is seen between the Wilford Lane and Wilford Village stops with a service for The Forest (terminating short due to problems on the northern section of the route) on the morning of 12 August 2021. The high fence to the left is designed to prevent balls and the like reaching the tramway from the various sports fields on this side of the line! To the right, the treeline marks the site of the former GC line formation. *Robert Pritchard*

**Left:** Clearly showing the straight nature of the route on the former GC railway alignment, 206 races a cyclist between the Compton Acres and Ruddington Lane stops with a service for Clifton South on 10 October 2021. *Ian Beardsley*

**Below:** 224 arrives at Ruddington Lane, where slab track is used, with a service for Clifton South on 17 July 2016. *Robert Pritchard*

by any trams turning back here, although none are scheduled to do so in normal service.

On leaving Clifton Centre we cross Green Lane at a busy interchange and continue on Southchurch Drive. The impressive Corpus Christi Roman Catholic Church is to our left. Another church, Holy Trinity, gives its name to the next stop. At the south end of Southchurch Drive we bear right and leave the street running section briefly, with Holy Trinity stop located on a brief off-street segregated section. The church is immediately opposite, alongside Clifton Police Station.

Leaving Holy Trinity we are back on street running, heading due west on Farnborough Road for the last leg of our journey to Clifton South. The large Clifton View Care Home lies to our right. The penultimate stop, almost within sight of the terminus, is Summerwood Lane, which is an island platform and is just before Summerwood Lane itself, which is on the left.

For the last leg of our journey we cross the tree-lined Nottingham Road and bear left, now on our own segregated alignment again for a very short distance, to terminate at Clifton South. This marks the end of the residential development and with open countryside to the

south and west the end of the line feels very much like a countryside terminus! The relatively new Lark Hill village development lies to the north and the stop is surrounded by another Park & Ride site with around 1000 parking spaces. The P&R site is signposted from Junction 24 of the M1 motorway and then accessed via the A453. In terms of the tramway infrastructure, there is a scissors crossover just before the terminus and trams will normally cross over before arrival and use the northside platform, which can accommodate

**Left:** With the tower block adjacent to the Southchurch Drive North stop visible behind, 227 is running through the rural section before trams join the former GC railway alignment with an afternoon service from Clifton South to Phoenix Park on 17 July 2016. *Robert Pritchard*

**Below:** On the rural section of the Clifton South route between Ruddington Lane and Southchurch Drive North, 211 passes the Silverdale Crossover and it heads towards the Clifton district on 10 October 2021. *Ian Beardsley*

**Left:** The tram tracks widen as 207 approaches the Clifton Centre stop with a service for Clifton South on 12 August 2021. *Robert Pritchard*

**Above:** The Corpus Christi Roman Catholic Church is to the right as 228 runs down Southchurch Drive, between the Clifton Centre and Holy Trinity stops, with a service for Clifton South on 12 August 2021.

**Above:** 236 runs down Farnborough Road with a service for Phoenix Park on 17 July 2016. *Robert Pritchard (2)*

**Above:** Having left Clifton South, trams enter a street-running section almost immediately, in contrast with departures from all of the other termini. On 12 August 2021 231 has just left the terminus and is crossing Nottingham Road, before running onto Farnborough Road with a service for The Forest (terminating short here due to overhead line problems in the Basford area on this day).

two trams (and is numbered "A" and "C"). The south side platform is numbered "B". The stop used to incorporate a small coffee shop/kiosk, as at Toton Lane, but this has now closed and this area is now used as a meeting place for community events.

Clifton South is the slightly shorter branch and has less street running than the Toton Lane line. From Sheriffs Way Junction to the terminus the Clifton South branch is 7.33 km and around two-thirds of that is on segregated track.

**Above:** 224 stands at the Clifton South terminus, in the usually served Platform "A" on 17 July 2016. *Robert Pritchard (2)*

## CHAPTER 4:

# THE NET TRAM FLEET

Today, Nottingham Express Transit has a fleet of 37 trams, the largest modern tram fleet of any of the UK systems after Manchester. There are two distinct designs of trams which are used interchangeably across the two routes. The original fleet consisted of 15 Bombardier Incentro AT6/5 five-section cars assembled at Bombardier Transportation's Derby Litchurch Lane Works, numbered 201–215. These are supplemented by 22 Alstom Citadis five-section trams, 216–237, which were delivered in 2013–14 ahead of the system's expansion.

The original trams are a variant of Bombardier's Incentro design (marketed as the ADtranz Incentro until the acquisition of ADtranz by Bombardier in 2001). 33 of the slightly earlier AT6/5L version were built for Nantes, France, for use on its expanded 41.4 km system to supplement older Alsthom trams built between 1984 and 1994 (trams had been reintroduced in Nantes in 1985). NET's AT6/5 is a shorter version of the Nantes AT6/5L with a length of 33 m (compared to 36.4 m for the AT6/5L). Both versions are five-section low-floor models, but the Nantes version has several key

**Above:** Nantes in France operates a fleet of 33 Bombardier Incentro trams which were built between 2000 and 2006. One of the original batch, 360, passes the château of the Ducs de Bretagne (Dukes of Brittany) just after Duchesse Anne station with a Line 1 service to François Mitterrand on 30 March 2010. *David Haydock*

interior differences including more longitudinal seating. Nantes's fleet of 33 Incentro trams were supplied in two batches, 23 in 2000–01 and ten in 2005–06, the latter just after Nottingham's fleet was delivered. It is worth noting that Nantes is a city of a very similar size to Nottingham.

**Below:** The original 15 Bombardier Incentro trams have carried a number of different advertising or promotional liveries, particularly during the 2010s. On 26 August 2013 204 approaches the Phoenix Park terminus wearing a striking "Glide into Nottingham" blue advertising livery, promoting the hop-on, hop-off bus, train and tram combined mode ticket. *Robert Pritchard*

**Left:** In the original livery, 203 is seen on Waverley Street passing The Arboretum with a service for Station Street on 9 March 2004, the first day of normal service. The outermost bogies are powered, and as typical for trams are covered by shields to protect the wheels. *Mike Haddon*

**Below:** It is quite often difficult to get photos of one of the Incentro trams without any adverts on at all. Recently refurbished and repainted into the second Incentro livery, 201 is seen here minus any advertising as it arrives at Old Market Square with a service for Station Street on 3 August 2014.

When NET was being planned in the late 1990s the original plan was to order a fleet of Eurotram light rail vehicles, originally manufactured by ABB Group at York Carriage Works and Derby Litchurch Lane, similar to those built at York and Derby for Strasbourg, France, and those assembled in Portugal from parts built in Derby for the Porto system. These were based on a prototype developed by Italian manufacturer Socimi. Versions of the Eurotram also operate in Milan, Italy. However, the Eurotram was found to be unsuitable for Nottingham for two reasons – the installed power was seen as insufficient for Nottingham's hills and the large single-leaf doors would take too long to

Some companies that previously had all-over advertising liveries still advertise on trams with partial adverts. One such company is e.on, with these adverts on 212 ("Nottingham it's time to clear the air"). The tram, in the third version of the standard NET livery, is seen leaving Cator Lane for Toton Lane on 12 August 2021. Later in 2021 this tram would receive a livery promoting Carbon Neutral Nottingham 2028. *Robert Pritchard (2)*

open and close, thus resulting in extended stop times and an unacceptable end-to-end journey time (and also would have required a larger tram fleet). After Bombardier acquired ABB Group's successor Adtranz, the Eurotram model was then marketed as part of Bombardier's Flexity Outlook family of trams.

### THE INCENTRO TRAM FOR NOTTINGHAM

The Incentro is a bi-directional vehicle with five articulated sections and two motor bogies (the two outermost bogies) and one trailer bogie under the middle section, which also includes a single-arm pantograph. Each motor bogie has four independently-rotating wheels, each powered by a water-cooled asynchronous traction motor, with automatic sanding. Resilient wheels are fitted, with flange lubrication on the centre bogie. With installed power of around 500 hp the trams are designed for a maximum gradient of around 1 in 12.

The bodies are fabricated in stainless steel with GRP cladding and an aluminium alloy roof. Side windows are single glazed with tinted glass and each tram has two passenger compartment air-conditioning units. Braking is regenerative and disc with the standard magnetic track brakes for emergency use. The trams have cameras mounted on both sides at both ends. These point back along the sides of the vehicle and give the driver a clear view of the doors and platform before they leave a stop, removing the need for mirrors. There are also CCTV cameras covering the passenger areas. There are four double sets of doors per side, plus two single doors at each end, next to the driver's cab. Three roof-mounted Passenger Information Screens are fitted per vehicle.

In terms of the interior, most of the 54 seats are laid out in a 2+2 facing layout but with a 2+1 layout in the centre section. The 2+2 layout did draw criticism for the narrow

**Above:** Car 209 is seen in one of the three original advertising liveries, for Westbury Homes. It is on "ghost running" on the approach to Wilkinson Street on 18 February 2004, just over two weeks before Phase 1 of NET opened. *Mike Haddon*

**Above:** 201 is carrying adverts for Nottingham Contemporary as it leaves Highbury Vale (Phoenix Park branch platforms) for Station Street on 26 August 2013. Several of the advertising liveries retained some elements of the fleet livery, such as here on the front ends.

aisles. Over the bogies the seats are mounted on plinths which can be more difficult to access for those with reduced mobility. There are also four tip-up seats and two designated wheelchair spaces. There are four "perch" rests too, two at each end facing inwards from the driving cab. Seats were initially finished in a plain cyan green upholstery which was later changed on refurbishment (see below). Maximum speed is 80 km/h, although this is only attained on some of the segregated sections. Street running sections are limited to 50 km/h, although in practice much lower speeds are more

**Left:** Wearing a striking red advertising livery for energy firm e.on with the byline "Putting our Energy into Nottingham", 208 has just left The Forest with a service for Station Street on 3 August 2014. *Robert Pritchard (2)*

usual, especially in the city centre. The full technical specification is shown in Table 2.

The first car, 201, was shown off to the railway media at Bombardier's Derby Works on 13 August 2002, with the then Minister for Transport John Spellar officially launching the tram before taking a ride on the 1 km factory test track. At this time trams 201–204 were complete with 205–207 under construction. The Incentro trams are notable as being the only modern trams in operation in the UK to be assembled at a UK factory, all other systems using cars imported from mainland Europe. Body parts were, however, fabricated in Amadora in Portugal (in a plant that specialises in stainless-steel construction) and the bogies made in

**Above:** In a lime green advert livery for Nottingham Express Transit's **thetram.net** website, 209 has just left Old Market Square as it heads for Station Street on 17 July 2016.

**Above:** Car 211 has carried the most advert liveries. In the Alstom light blue colours the tram has just left Phoenix Park for Station Street on 30 December 2014.

Germany, with final assembly, interior fit out and testing taking place at Derby. They were also the first 100% low-floor trams to operate in the UK. The number series 201–215 follows on from Nottingham's old trams which were numbered up to 200.

Car 202 was the first to be delivered to Wilkinson Street depot in Nottingham in October 2002 and testing within the confines of the depot started in January 2003.

## LIVERIES

In terms of liveries, during their near 20-year life the Incentro trams have now carried three different fleet liveries plus numerous advertising liveries. The original fleet livery was a mix of dark green (lower bodyside), a silver stripe, black window surrounds and silver band at the top. The green was chosen as it recalled the predominant historic colour used by Nottingham City Transport on buses and trolleybuses.

After the change of operating concession and during the first refurbishment in 2013–14 (see below) a different livery was applied, with more silver than green but still with black window surrounds. During the mid-life overhaul in 2019–21 a third livery was applied that more closely resembled that given to the Citadis fleet, returning to being mainly dark green, particularly along the top of the tram.

Advertising liveries have been an important part of NET since the beginning, also bringing in some additional revenue and leading to some very colourful trams to photograph. Three trams – 201, 209 and 213 – were in advertising liveries for the start of operation and in total ten of the original 15 Bombardier trams have carried full all-over adverts – a full list is shown in Table 1. 211 has carried the most – five different advert liveries. Only the Incentros have ever carried advert liveries, never any of the Citadis cars. At some times several trams could be seen in different liveries, but in 2019 NET announced that following the

**Right:** In a colourful lime green, blue and purple advert livery for Deliveroo, 211 runs onto the Wilford Bridge with a service for Phoenix Park on 9 April 2019. *Robert Pritchard (3)*

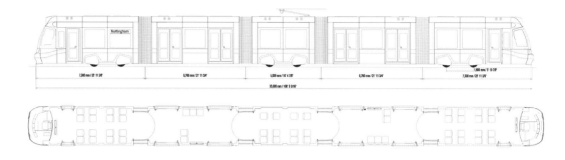

**Above:** Line drawing of the Bombardier Incentro for Nottingham. *Courtesy Bombardier*

second refurbishment of these cars and repainting of the fleet only a maximum of two trams would carry all-over advert liveries at any one time in future – at the request of the city council.

There was then a period for most of 2021 when there were no all-over advert liveries, until 212 emerged in a Carbon Neutral Nottingham scheme in November 2021. This promoted the city's pledge to become the country's first carbon neutral city by 2028.

This was also notable as being 212's first advertising livery. 212 was unveiled on 29 November 2021 at Wilkinson Street depot by two young pupils (Alfie Daniels and Ariadne Van Krimpen) from Alderman Pounder Infant and Nursery School who were selected as the city's first "Trambassadors", acting as an important community link for NET and providing STEM-based learning opportunities for children. CEO of Tramlink Tim Hesketh said: "Nottingham is leading the charge in tackling climate change so this newly wrapped tram will create a 'green symbol' of the city's clean growth ambitions. We are proud to be a central part of the 'Carbon Neutral 2028' campaign and delighted that our young Trambassadors helped unveil the new look tram as we work together to build a greener future for Nottingham."

Many cars have also carried partial adverts, particularly along the roofline, or full advertising just on the shorter middle section. Notably, in 2020, 204 was given multi-coloured partial adverts celebrating the work of keyworkers during the coronavirus pandemic.

**Above:** 207 is carrying a white and yellow advert livery for PayPoint top-ups as it arrives at The Forest for Station Street on 3 August 2014.

**Right:** Carrying the colourful Just Eat livery, 210 arrives at Nottingham Station with a service for Clifton South on 30 June 2018. *Robert Pritchard (2)*

**Above:** In Jet2 advertising livery, 206 passes Sheriffs Way Junction, where the Clifton South and Toton Lane lines diverge on a street running section not far from Nottingham Station, with a service bound for Toton Lane on 9 April 2019.

## TABLE I. INCENTRO ADVERTISING LIVERIES

| Car | Advert | Dates carried |
|---|---|---|
| 201 | Powergen (two versions – green or blue) | 2004–2008 |
| | Mynottinghamjobs.co.uk (orange & white) | 2008–2009 |
| | NET celebrating 5 years (blue) | 2009 |
| | Nottinghamcontemporary.org (yellow, blue & white) | 2009–2014 |
| 204 | NET Glide into Nottingham (blue) | 2012–2013 |
| 206 | e.on (red) | 2013–2016 |
| | jet2.com (red & blue) | 2016–2019 |
| 207 | The Snowman (indigo) | 2013–2014 |
| | PayPoint (white & yellow) | 2014–2016 |
| 208 | e.on (red) | 2012–2014 |
| 209 | Westbury Homes (blue) | 2004–2007 |
| | Interski (white & blue) | 2013–2014 |
| | Various NET/Trent Barton/Big Event ticket promotions (lime green) | 2014–2021 |
| 210 | Just Eat (various colours) | 2017–2019 |
| 211 | NET Tram It (various colours) | 2010–2012 |
| | Queen's Diamond Jubilee (red) | 2012–2013 |
| | Nottingham Armed Forces Day (red) | 2013 |
| | Alstom (light blue) | 2013–2016 |
| | Deliveroo (green, blue & purple) | 2016–2019 |
| 212 | Carbon Neutral Nottingham 2028 (white, green & blue) | 2021–present |
| 213 | Powergen (two versions – green or blue) | 2004–2007 |
| | e.on clean air (red) | 2020–2021 |

**Above:** The most recent advertising livery on NET as this book was being prepared was this Carbon Neutral Nottingham 2028 livery on car 212, which still carries its "William Booth" name, but with no external numbers. It is seen at Royal Centre with a service for Clifton South on 11 December 2021. *Robert Pritchard (2)*

### INCENTRO REFURBISHMENT

In December 2012 NET announced that the Incentro fleet was to be refurbished as well as receiving a new exterior livery. The interior, now starting to look a little tired after nine years of intensive use, was refreshed, with new bright green upholstery with lime green lining, the same as was fitted to the new Citadis trams that were by then under construction. The work also included fitting new energy-efficient LED lighting. Work on refurbishing the first car, 215, started in early 2013 and it re-entered service on 8 March 2013. All 15

*Above:* The original Incentro interior, showing one of the centre sections with a wheelchair space and two tip-up seats to the left and three longitudinal seats to the right. *Peter Fox*

*Above & Below:* Two views of the refurbished interior of car 203, showing (above) the 2+1 layout in the centre section with the seats mounted on plinths over where the bogies are and (below) the wheelchair area and two tip-up seats which are located in sections 2 and 4. *Robert Pritchard (2)*

*Above:* Original interior of Incentro car 202 looking down the full length of the tram.

*Above:* The cab control panel at the "B" end of Incentro car 202. *Mike Haddon (2)*

cars had been refurbished by the middle of 2014. The eighth car to be refurbished (211) took longer than the others as it was fitted with a prototype Automatic Vehicle Location System (signalling and tram communication system) that was later rolled out across the whole fleet.

This work was followed by a £3.5 million mid-life rebuild which started with car 203 in early 2019. The rebuild was aimed at improving reliability, comfort and accessibility. It included a complete strip out of the trams and the flooring and interior fittings were replaced and all cars were also given a full mechanical overhaul. The door open/close buttons were replaced with more modern versions. For passengers there was little change after this work – the seating layout has been kept the same, with the same upholstery used as in the first refurbishment. Car 203 was relaunched by the Sheriff of Nottingham Cllr Catharine Arnold in a special event at the depot on 10 May 2019.

The original plan was that the mid-life rebuild work would be completed by the end of 2020 but delays, not least caused by delays in the supply of materials and the effects of the Covid-19 pandemic on the workforce, meant that the last tram – 214 – was not released until 22 March 2021.

## TABLE 2. BOMBARDIER INCENTRO TECHNICAL DATA

| | |
|---|---|
| Built | 2002–03 by Bombardier, Derby, England |
| Number series | 201–215 |
| Wheel arrangement | Bo-2-Bo |
| Traction motors | 8 x 45 kW (65 hp) wheelmotors |
| Line voltage | 750 V DC |
| Track gauge | 1435 mm |
| Seats | 54+4 tip-up |
| Total passenger capacity (4 pass/m²) | 193 |
| Total passenger capacity (6 pass/m²) | 261 |
| Weight | 36.7 tonnes |
| Braking | Disc, regenerative and magnetic track |
| Wheel diameter (new) | 660 mm |
| Couplers | Not equipped |
| Maximum speed | 80 km/h (50 mph) |
| Doors | Sliding plug |
| **DIMENSIONS** | |
| Length | 33.0 m |
| Width | 2.40 m |
| Height (with pantograph lowered) | 3.35 m |
| PERFORMANCE DATA | |
| Service acceleration rate | 1.2 m/s² |
| Deceleration (service brake) | 1.4 m/s² |
| Deceleration (emergency brakes) | 2.5 m/s² |

## THE ALSTOM CITADIS TRAMS

A further batch of trams was needed for the Phase 2 lines and by the time Phase 2 was being planned and constructed the Bombardier Incentro design was no longer available. With Alstom winning a 22½ year maintenance contract for the NET fleet in December 2011 it was no surprise that the Alstom Citadis design was chosen and on 15 December 2011 a fleet of 22 cars were ordered. Designs for the new trams were unveiled in May 2012, with a very similar look to the Citadis in use in Dublin. The Citadis is a modular design of mainly aluminium construction using standardised components but adapted for each system (the front end design is often changed for different systems). The modular design means that trams could be lengthened by inserting more middle sections, which has happened with much of the Citadis fleet in Dublin (but is unlikely to happen in Nottingham because of infrastructure constraints). Ironically Bombardier Transportation, which built NET's Incentro fleet, has itself been owned by Alstom – builder of the Citadis fleet – since January 2021.

The Nottingham cars are Citadis Type 302, a five-section car quite closely resembling the Incentros in terms of its dimensions and many of the technical characteristics but specially adapted for Nottingham Express Transit. Both the Incentro and the Citadis are unique to NET as far as the UK is concerned but versions of the Citadis can be found on the Luas network in Dublin, Ireland,

**Below:** The Alstom Citadis is a modular design supplied by Alstom to a number of cities in mainland Europe, particularly France. Dijon has a system of a similar size to NET with a fleet of 33 five-section Citadis 302 cars similar to those used in Nottingham. On 10 September 2014 car 1001 is seen shortly after departing from the terminus at Chenôve on Line 2 in the south of the city. Note the grassed track, a common feature of many of the French tramways. *Alan Yearsley*

**Left:** The first of the Alstom trams, car 216, was delivered to the Wilkinson Street depot on 10 September 2013 and was displayed to local and trade media in a launch event three days later.

**Below:** Local dignitaries including NET General Manager Paul Robinson, Portfolio Holder for Planning and Transport at Nottingham City Council Councillor Jane Urquhart, Lord Mayor of Nottingham Councillor Merlita Bryan, Alstom UK President Terence Watson and staff from the depot line up in front of newly arrived Citadis car 216 at the press launch event on 13 September 2013. *Robert Pritchard (2)*

and on many other light rail networks throughout the world including (to name but a few) Algiers, Algeria; Rio de Janeiro, Brazil; Ottawa, Canada; Shanghai, China; and several networks in France such as Angers, Bordeaux, Dijon, Lyon, Montpellier, and Orléans. In total (at the time of writing) more than 2600 Alstom Citadis trams have been sold to more than 50 cities on five continents across the world.

The first of the 22 trams, car 216, was delivered to Wilkinson Street depot on the evening of 10 September 2013 and unveiled to local and trade media during a well-attended press launch on 13 September. During this event Terence Watson, Alstom UK President, handed over the keys for 216 to the Lord Mayor of Nottingham, Councillor Merlita Bryan. It was also announced at the event that the Citadis trams had a design life of 35 years and each was forecast to run around 90 000 km annually.

The new trams were constructed at Alstom's Santa Perpetua (Barcelona) factory. The first was extensively tested at Alstom's La Rochelle test facility in France before being shipped to the UK via the Port of Southampton. The remainder were shipped direct

**Left:** The Alstom Citadis trams for Nottingham were shipped to the Port of Southampton from Barcelona (apart from the first, which was shipped from La Rochelle). The second to arrive, 217, is seen on Town Quay, Southampton on 10 October 2013 at the start of its journey north by road to Nottingham – it would be delivered to the depot at Wilkinson Street later that day. *Graham Tiller*

every two weeks giving Nottingham six new trams (216–221) by the end of 2013. 222 was delivered on 19 January 2014 and deliveries then took place every two to three weeks (and at sometimes more frequent intervals) until November 2014. The final car, 237, was delivered on 14 November 2014 and an official ceremony took place ten days later at Wilkinson Street depot with NET and Alstom staff to mark the completion of the deliveries.

Continuing the practice of numbering its trams in series after the former Nottingham Corporation trams, the new trams received the numbers 216–237. The initial deliveries caused some confusion as the only external numbering was actually the delivery sequence numbers, for example 216 carried a tiny "001" on the upper bodyside, above the front doors. The fleet number was also later applied alongside this, on the CCTV

from Barcelona to Southampton and then moved by road to Wilkinson Street depot.

Like the Incentros there are five sections with three bogies, the two outermost being motored. Each motor axle has two 120 kW water-cooled traction motors and is independent in motoring. The pantograph is fitted to the centre (trailer) section and the door arrangement is the same as on the Incentros. The Citadis cars are fully low-floor and are slightly shorter than the Incentros but have more seats (58 plus ten tip-ups). The main change in terms of the interior is that the layout in the centre section is 2+2 rather than 2+1. There are also tip-up seats in some of the doorways, unlike the Incentros, but there are no perch rests at the ends. With more seats the overall seating and standing capacity – at 216 – is slightly less than the Incentros. Maximum speed is 70 km/h, less than the 80 km/h of the Incentros. The full technical specification is shown in Table 3.

The second tram to be delivered was 217 on 10 October 2013. Delivery of the following four trams took place roughly

**Above:** Showing the Alstom Citadis roof detail, 236 runs up the ramp into the Nottingham Station stop with a Clifton South–Phoenix Park service on 17 July 2016. *Robert Pritchard (3)*

camera. To make identification easier, in 2016 much larger fleet numbers were applied on the front ends above the windscreen. Some of the delivery sequence numbers (001–022) have now been removed but many are still also carried.

Testing of the Citadis fleet was initially conducted within the boundaries of the depot before overnight testing started on the Hucknall route. Overnight street testing into the city centre using 216 and 218 started in November 2013. Trials then moved to daytime testing, commissioning and driver training from April 2014. Each tram had to complete 1000 km of fault free miles before being accepted for traffic.

In terms of service introduction there was a "big bang" introduction on Sunday 27 July 2014 as part of a trial for a new higher frequency timetable for the Phase 1 routes to provide more capacity. Six of the Citadis trams all entered service on this date (216–221), with 218 being the first to carry passengers. 216 had to be withdrawn from service during the morning with a door fault, but it returned to service later in the day. No further trams entered service in 2014, but by April 2015 the first ten, 216–225, were all in traffic and the last cars entered service by the time the new extensions opened on 25 August 2015.

**Above:** Front end detail on Citadis car 231 (while paused at the Rivergreen stop) showing the large number above the cab applied in 2016 and to the right the much smaller number 231 and alongside that the number "016" – this was the delivery sequence number of this car (the 16th of the Citadis trams to be delivered). Also seen is the name "Rebecca Adlington OBE" and the prominent Alstom logo.

**Above:** Showing its "flute like" end to good effect, 223 leaves the Bramcote Lane stop in glorious early evening light on 17 July 2016 with a service for Toton Lane. *Robert Pritchard (2)*

**Above:** Interior of car 216 taken from the front section looking towards the middle of the tram.

**Above:** Two of the key differences from the Incentros are seen here – two of the tip-up seats next to the doors and the 2+2 layout in the centre section (as opposed to 2+1 in the Incentros).

**Above:** One of the two areas for wheelchairs in the Citadis cars. *Robert Pritchard (3)*

The Citadis fleet has always carried the same livery since introduction, and has not carried any external advertising.

### TABLE 3. ALSTOM CITADIS TECHNICAL DATA

| | |
|---|---|
| Built | 2013–14 by Alstom, Barcelona, Spain |
| Number series | 216–237 |
| Wheel arrangement | Bo-2-Bo |
| Traction motors | 4 x 120 kW (161 hp) |
| Line voltage | 750 V DC |
| Track gauge | 1435 mm |
| Seats | 58+10 tip-up |
| Total passenger capacity (4 pass/m²) | 144 |
| Total passenger capacity (6 pass/m²) | 216 |
| Weight | 40.8 tonnes |
| Braking | Disc, regenerative and magnetic track |
| Couplers | Not equipped |
| Maximum speed | 70 km/h (43 mph) |
| Doors | Sliding plug |
| **DIMENSIONS** | |
| Length | 32.0 m |
| Width | 2.40 m |
| Height (with pantograph lowered) | 3.45 m |
| **PERFORMANCE DATA** | |
| Service acceleration rate | 1.18 m/s² |

### NAMES: INCENTRO FLEET

The entire NET tram fleet carries the names of people famously associated with the city or local area and also well-known community campaigners. The names are displayed on vinyl transfers beneath the side window of the driving cab on the right-hand side as you look towards the cab end on the Incentros and (in most cases) on all four corners of the Citadis cars. Many of the names were voted for by viewers of the BBC's regional news programme East Midlands Today or by listeners of local radio stations such as Trent FM and BBC Radio Nottingham. Nine of the 15 Incentros were named in a ceremony on 1 July 2004, with the remainder having their names applied by the middle of that month. They were named after a mix of living legends of Nottinghamshire such as Torvill & Dean, local historical figures such as William Booth and local unsung heroes such as Sidney Standard.

The Incentros have carried the same names, although some have lost them for a time on one side, sometimes as a result of a graffiti attack.

**Above:** The cab layout at the "B" end of Citadis car 222, with the combined power/brake handle to the left.

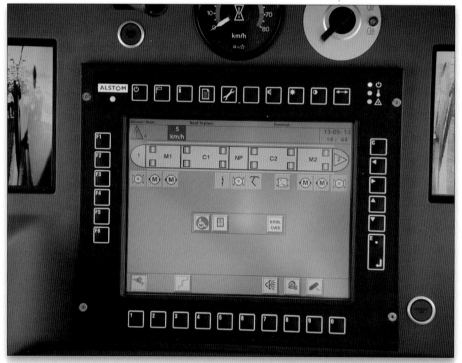

**Above:** The information screen for the driver in the cab of 216 showing a layout of the five section car.
*Robert Pritchard (2)*

### NAMES: ALSTOM CITADIS FLEET

A new competition for a further series of names was run as the larger fleet of Citadis was being delivered: a special online form was launched during 2015 to give NET passengers and other members of the public the opportunity to put forward their suggested names. NET

Marketing Manager Jamie Swift commented at the time: "Obviously, many more people use the internet now than they did in 2004 when NET tram services were launched. By collecting suggestions online we hope even more local people will get involved in the naming process."

Unlike the Incentros, three of the Citadis trams have carried more than one name. Until 2019 two trams were designated either "Nurse of the year tram" or "community star tram", with the aim being that two trams would be renamed annually to recognise the Nottingham Nurse and Midwife of the Year (which was sponsored by NET from 2014) and also after local community heroes.

216 became the first Citadis tram to be named in July 2014 when it was given the name "Julie Poulter" to recognise that year's Nurse of the Year. The following year 216 was given the permanent name "Dame Laura Knight", however, and 220 then became Nurse of the Year tram. It carried five different names between 2015 and 2019 (Table 5). The 2019 winner Sophie Robson was carried until late 2021 when 220 was given a new more permanent name to honour Sir Martyn Poliakoff. 222, meanwhile, was the community star tram and it carried four names between 2015 and 2018 (three of these including two people) before being given the more permanent name "David S Stewart OBE" in 2019. In early 2022 a new competition was launched by NET and the Nottingham Post to find a new "Community Hero", with a tram

## TABLE 4. INCENTRO NAMES

| Car | Name | Who is the tram named after? |
|---|---|---|
| 201 | Torvill & Dean | Olympic Gold Medal figure skating champions Jayne Torvill and Christopher Dean are Britain's best known ice skaters. Both were born in Nottingham |
| 202 | DH Lawrence | The Eastwood-born novelist whose publications include The White Peacock, Sons And Lovers, and Lady Chatterley's Lover |
| 203 | Bendigo Thompson | The bare-knuckle fighter William "Bendigo" Thompson who achieved Champion of England fame in 1835 |
| 204 | Erica Beardsmore | A Hyson Green-based supporter of Nottingham In Bloom |
| 205 | Lord Byron | The Nottinghamshire-born romantic poet and politician |
| 206 | Angela Alcock | A local Oxfam donations collector who collected many thousands of pounds for the charity over the years she was involved |
| 207 | Mavis Worthington | A Homestart volunteer. Homestart is a charity which befriends families with young children and gives support in times of need |
| 208 | Dinah Minton | Founder of the Headway charity in the late 1970s and led a campaign which involves getting better treatment for victims who have survived surgery |
| 209 | Sidney Standard | (originally Sid Standard), former owner of a bike shop on Chilwell Road, Beeston. He is thought to have travelled more than half a million miles on his bike whilst introducing others to the activity |
| 210 | Sir Jesse Boot | The founder of Boots the Chemist, he was given the Freedom of Nottingham City in 1920 |
| 211 | Robin Hood | The famous legendary outlaw long associated with Nottingham and the nearby Sherwood Forest who was famous for robbing the rich to feed the poor and fighting against injustice and tyranny |
| 212 | William Booth | Sneinton born, Booth was founder of the East London Christian Mission (later renamed the Salvation Army) |
| 213 | Mary Potter | Founder of the Sisters of the Little Company of Mary, a Roman Catholic religious institute founded in Hyson Green and dedicated to caring for the suffering, the sick and the dying |
| 214 | Dennis McCarthy, MBE | A former BBC Radio Nottingham presenter who spent 25 years broadcasting to the city |
| 215 | Brian Clough OBE | A former footballer and manager of Nottingham Forest FC from 1975 to 1993 |

due to be named in March 2022 to mark NET's 18th anniversary. Retiring Deputy Chief Medical Officer Professor Sir Jonathan Van-Tam was widely expected to be one of the top contenders to win the competition, but it was not announced which tram would be renamed.

Some additional suffixes have been needed where people have later been given knighthoods after the original naming. For example, cricketer Stuart Broad was given an MBE after he helped England regain the Ashes from Australia in summer 2015 and the letters "MBE" were added after his name in 2016.

**Above & right:** NET trams, usually car 220, have carried six different names honouring Nottingham's Nurse or Midwife of the Year, which was organised by Nottingham University Hospitals NHS Trust and the Nottingham Post, with NET being headline sponsors until 2019. The most recent nurse to be honoured was Sophie Robson, who unveiled her name on 220 on 17 December 2019. 220 was renamed Sir Martyn Poliakoff in 2021. *Robert Pritchard (top photo)/ Courtesy NET (right)*

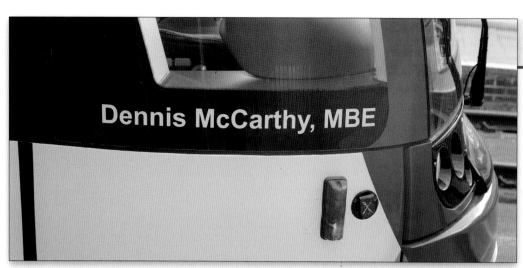

**Left:** The only name to include any punctuation is 214 "Dennis McCarthy, MBE". *Robert Pritchard*

## TABLE 5. CITADIS NAMES

| Car | Name | Who is the tram named after? |
|-----|------|------------------------------|
| 216[1] | Dame Laura Knight | A Long Eaton-born artist, one of the most famous female artists of her time in Britain |
| 217 | Carl Froch | A Nottingham-born former professional heavyweight boxer who became WBA unified champion in 2013 |
| 218 | Jim Taylor | The former Director of Development at Nottingham City Council, who was heavily involved in the development of the NET project and redevelopment of Old Market Square |
| 219 | Alan Sillitoe | A Nottingham-born writer who was awarded honorary degrees by both Nottingham Polytechnic (now Nottingham Trent University) and the University of Nottingham |
| 220[2] | Professor Sir Martyn Poliakoff | The most recent name, applied in December 2021 to honour Poliakoff, a pioneering scientist and global leader in green and sustainable chemistry. He is known for his series of YouTube videos called Periodic Table of Videos, which started out from the University of Nottingham's School of Chemistry and now have a global audience |
| 221 | Stephen Lowe | A playwright and director from Sneinton |
| 222[3] | David S Stewart OBE | Former Head of Oak Field special school in Bilborough. Mr Stewart was previously Head of the now-closed Shepherd School and was awarded an OBE for services to education in 2003 |
| 223 | Colin Slater MBE | A long-serving Notts County FC commentator for BBC Radio Nottingham, who has covered over 2000 Notts County matches for the radio station |
| 224 | Vicky McClure | A Nottingham-based actress known for her roles as Detective Inspector Kate Fleming in the BBC series Line of Duty and Lol Jenkins in Shane Meadows's film and TV series This is England |
| 225 | Doug Scott CBE | A Nottingham-born mountaineer who was the first English person (along with Dougal Haston) to reach the summit of Mount Everest |
| 226 | Jimmy Sirrel & Jack Wheeler | Jimmy Sirrel was Manager of Notts County FC on three occasions between 1969 and 1987, and Jack Wheeler was the club's Caretaker Manager in 1968–69 and held a number of other roles including Coach, Trainer and Scout. Sirrel and Wheeler are widely regarded as Notts County's greatest ever management team, who led the club to a number of achievements including promotion to the First Division in 1981 |
| 227 | Sir Peter Mansfield | A physicist and Professor of Physics at the University of Nottingham. One of the world's most celebrated scientists, he played a key role in the invention of the MRI scanner |
| 228 | Local Armed Forces | Named on Remembrance Day in 2015 in honour of Heroes Nottingham service personnel who gave their lives in the two World Wars and more recent conflicts |
| 229 | Viv Anderson MBE | A football coach and former Nottingham Forest player who was born in Clifton |
| 230 | George Green | A Sneinton-born mathematical physicist who received only one year of formal schooling as a child and was largely self-taught |
| 231 | Rebecca Adlington OBE | A competitive swimmer from Mansfield who won two gold medals at 2008 Beijing Olympics, breaking the World Record for the 800 m freestyle. She went on to become a swimming pundit for BBC TV |
| 232 | William Ivory | A theatre writer and actor long associated with the Nottingham Playhouse who created the 1990s BBC comedy drama series Common as Muck and the 2010 film Made in Dagenham |
| 233 | Ada Lovelace | The daughter of the poet Lord Byron and an inspirational female figurehead whose work is said to have included the world's first computer programming around 100 years ahead of its time |
| 234 | George Africanus | A West African former slave who became a successful entrepreneur in Nottingham |
| 235 | David Clarke | A former Nottingham Panthers captain and one of the UK's most successful ice hockey players |
| 236 | Sat Bains | Satwant Singh "Sat" Bains is a Derby-born chef who is best known as the chef proprietor of the two-Michelin star Restaurant Sat Bains with Rooms in Nottingham |
| 237 | Stuart Broad MBE | A Nottingham-born cricketer who plays Test cricket for England and also for Nottinghamshire County Cricket Club |

**Previous names:**

[1] 216 originally named Julie Poulter (Nurse of the Year 2014).

[2] 220 carried Nurse of the Year winners from 2015 to 2019: Kim Helm (applied in 2015), Aprille Jones (2016), Christina O'Loughlin (2017), Luisa Avanzado (2018) and Sophie Robson (2019).

[3] 222 carried "community star" winners from 2015 to 2018: Sam & Amy (applied in 2015), Barbara White OBE (2016), Michelle and Richard Daniels (2017) and Tim and Jean Jeffrey (2018).

CHAPTER 5:

# THE DEPOT & INFRASTRUCTURE

Nottingham Express Transit is operated out of a single maintenance and administrative headquarters at Wilkinson Street. Built on decontaminated industrial land (a former gasworks) between the former Shipstone's Brewery and Cusson's soap factory the site includes a depot – significantly expanded to accommodate the new trams introduced in 2014–15, control centre and a number of offices, staff accommodation, administrative and customer services centres. The depot site includes an automatic tram wash, workshops for heavy repairs, a wheel lathe, sanding facilities and a driver's signing-on point and mess room – all drivers sign on for the start of a shift here. The Wilkinson Street site is located at the northern end of the Phase 1 street running section, alongside a Park & Ride site. The proximity of the Park & Ride means that enthusiasts can get a good view of trams stabled in the depot yard from the car park!

## THE NET DEPOT

An integral building houses the control centre and customer services on one side and the four-road depot building on the other. The original depot just had just two maintenance roads but the significant expansion of the fleet (from 15 to 37 trams) as part of the Phase 2 extensions led to an expansion of the depot, with another workshop road and eight additional outside stabling sidings.

The workshop now has three pitted roads where staff can undertake major maintenance: Road 1 is an unwired maintenance road with pits and has Incentro jacks at the north end and the wheel lathe at the south end – trams are shunted onto this road by a resident

Niteq 800-e battery-operated shunting locomotive. Road 2 has Citadis tram jacks on the north end and has high-level gantries and a pit on the south end. Road 3 has pits and gantries at both ends which were an addition for the new trams. Road 4, to the left of the building as viewing it from the Wilkinson Street tram stop, is the sanding bay.

Stabling berths alongside the shed run from 5 to 17. Roads 5–16 are the main storage roads. Roads 5–10 each have berths for three trams (split into south, middle and north, for example numbered 5S, 5M and 5N). 5N is used as a deep cleaning bay. Road 11 has an extra berth so can fit four trams. Roads 12–14 have three berths each and Roads 15–16 have two (north and south). Road 17 is not really a stabling berth – it is a stub siding only connected at one end and more often used to place trams that have a defect or may have been involved in an accident and are awaiting parts. There is space for two trams in Road 17 and this is also where deliveries of trams to or from the depot by road can take place.

The tram workshops are operated by Alstom as part of the current operating consortium and staff are kept busy with both routine maintenance and heavy repairs of the fleet of 37 NET trams. Alstom had been maintaining both its own trams and those manufactured by Bombardier, but in 2021 Alstom itself took over Bombardier. There

**Below:** Nottingham Express Transit's headquarters at Wilkinson Street depot on 23 September 2019, with Citadis trams 235 and 222 stabled outside on Roads 17 and 5 respectively and Incentro 206 just visible inside the depot on Road 2. *Robert Pritchard*

Construction of the depot at Wilkinson Street started in 2001. In this 20 April 2002 view the depot building is nearing completion and the depot yard area awaits the commencement of track laying.

purchasing power if possible and bring the relatively high cost of spares for these ageing trams down. If NET needs a major order for spares then it puts out a request to Nantes (which operates a somewhat larger fleet of 33 Incentros) to ask them if there is anything it wants to tag on to the orders. The European supply chain was changing as a result of Brexit, however, and NET was – where possible – trying to develop new relationships with UK suppliers. This includes Dorlec of Clay Cross which is now contracted to undertake all Incentro traction motor gearbox repairs, whilst the braking systems are overhauled by a firm in Manchester.

NET has around 180 drivers (out of its total of circa 300 staff). In normal circumstances

**Below:** Tracklaying and overhead line work is under way in the depot complex on 22 November 2002. *Mike Haddon (2)*

are four teams of six staff to keep the depot operating 24 hours a day, seven days a week. They are responsible for everything from planned maintenance, tyre turning and tyre changing, modification programmes, mid-life refurbishments and crash and accident damage as well as maintaining the wheel lathe and lifting equipment at the depot. Deep cleans of each tram are also carried out every six months.

There are differences with the two types of trams in terms of their maintenance requirements. In terms of lifting a tram, the Incentros need six jacks to lift the entire vehicle up using the bogie centres and the Citadis need 12 jacks to lift the bodyshells. At the time of my visit in 2019 the mid-life refurbishment of the Incentro trams was in full swing. As discussed in Chapter 4, the Incentro is not a standardised and universal design like the Citadis and only Nottingham and Nantes in France operate this design – as a result many of the parts are bespoke. Our guide at the depot explained that NET is in regular contact with Nantes on the acquisition of spares so the two operators can have joint

no more than five hours of continuous driving is allowed (or six in an emergency situation). The same drivers who drive trams out in service are also responsible for on-depot driving, from arriving on the depot to shutting the tram down. For arriving trams the control room authorises all moves so when an incoming tram arrives at either Wilkinson Street (trams arriving from the north) or Shipstone Street (trams arriving from the south or city centre) stops the driver is sent a depot entry request on his or her screen. The control centre will then give permission to enter the depot. Generally permission will be given to enter Road 4: drivers will either be asked to fill the sand boxes with sand or visually check the sand status of the tram and then to call the control centre back. Once this is done permission can be given to leave Road 4 and proceed through the tram wash

**Left:** During an early press visit to the Wilkinson Street depot in the year before the tramway opened, 211 is seen lifted on jacks on 16 July 2003. *Peter Fox*

**Right:** Work to extend the depot for the larger fleet is visible as 205 exits the site on 26 August 2013 and takes the line towards the Wilkinson Street stop. *Robert Pritchard*

at the back of the depot and then round the balloon loop and onto a specific stabling road on Roads 5–16. From arriving on the depot to stabling should normally take around 15 minutes. At night, nightstaff on the depot are responsible for prepping trams for service, and can also assist with sanding.

**Below:** The Wilkinson Street depot extension under construction on 10 March 2014. A view of the completed extended section of the depot building on the north side can be seen on page 77.

Also based at the depot are a fleet of ancillary vehicles. this includes a permaquip overhead line inspection vehicle affectionately known as "Wee Beastie" and a road-rail Unimog which is used for overhead line repair work or may also be used for snow clearing using a special attachment.

**Below:** Eight new sidings were laid at Wilkinson Street depot to accommodate the expanded fleet, as seen on 10 March 2014 with four newly delivered Citadis trams stabled. *Mike Haddon (2)*

**Left:** The depot plan in the Control Centre showing the status of the fleet on 23 September 2019. 32 trams are shown to be in service with the remaining five on the depot – 222 is the hot spare, 201, 206 and 212 are in the workshops and 235 is stabled on Road 17.

**Right:** The wheel lathe is located on Road 1 of the depot workshops. It was supplied by Talgo and is used for reprofiling wheels and flanges without having to remove them from the tram.

**Below:** Incentros 212 and 201 are undergoing attention in the depot on 23 September 2019 – 212 was in for its mid-life refurbishment and 201 for a bogie overhaul. *Robert Pritchard (3)*

**Above:** The body of the pioneer of the modern Nottingham tram fleet, Incentro 201, lifted without its bogies on 23 September 2019.

**Left:** 206 on Road 2 on 23 September 2019 showing the overhead gantries for access to the roof. This was the third tram to be refurbished and following completion of its refurbishment was on a "C" exam before being accepted back into traffic.

**Right:** The heavily stripped out interior of car 212 during its mid-life refurbishment, showing the extent of the work undertaken. *Robert Pritchard (3)*

**Above:** At the back of the depot is the tram wash, through which each tram arriving on the depot will run before using the balloon loop. It is very rare to see a dirty NET tram!

**Above:** Also stabled at the back of the depot is this self-propelled Permaquip PL067 Overhead Line Inspection Vehicle, named "Wee Beastie".

**Left:** NET's road-rail Unimog is seen outside the depot on 23 September 2019. It carries the EVN number 99 70 9 979035-1. *Robert Pritchard (3)*

## THE CONTROL CENTRE

Also based at Wilkinson Street is the NET control centre, the real hub of the operation on a day-to-day basis. This was significantly upgraded and re-equipped before the Phase 2 extensions opened in 2015. More than 180 CCTV cameras located at stops and beside help points across the expanded network feed HD digital images that can be viewed on a bank of 12 x 55 in flat screen monitors in the control room, as well as at individual workstations. The feed normally cycles between individual cameras and can be manually controlled. It also covers cameras at the Park & Ride sites that are operated by NET. In addition the control room has a large screen that monitors the

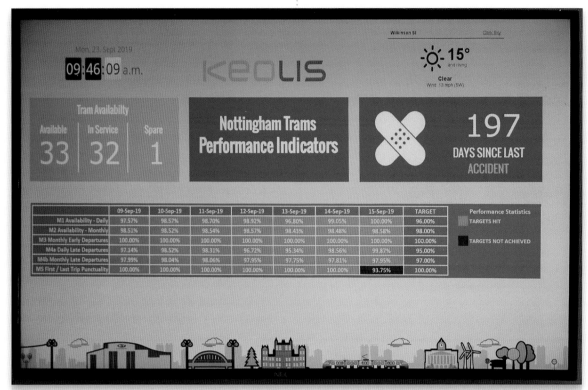

Mon, 23. Sept 2019

**09:46:09 a.m.**

**KEOLIS**

Wilkinson St — Clark Sky

☀ **15°**
and rising
**Clear**
Wind 13 mph (SW)

**Tram Availability**

| Available | In Service | Spare |
|-----------|-----------|-------|
| **33** | **32** | **1** |

**Nottingham Trams Performance Indicators**

**197 DAYS SINCE LAST ACCIDENT**

| | 09-Sep-19 | 10-Sep-19 | 11-Sep-19 | 12-Sep-19 | 13-Sep-19 | 14-Sep-19 | 15-Sep-19 | TARGET |
|---|---|---|---|---|---|---|---|---|
| M1 Availability - Daily | 97.57% | 98.57% | 98.70% | 98.92% | 96.80% | 99.05% | 100.00% | 96.00% |
| M2 Availability - Monthly | 98.51% | 98.52% | 98.54% | 98.57% | 98.43% | 98.48% | 98.58% | 98.00% |
| M3 Monthly Early Departures | 100.00% | 100.00% | 100.00% | 100.00% | 100.00% | 100.00% | 100.00% | 100.00% |
| M4a Daily Late Departures | 97.14% | 98.52% | 98.31% | 96.72% | 95.34% | 98.56% | 99.87% | 95.00% |
| M4b Monthly Late Departures | 97.99% | 98.04% | 98.06% | 97.95% | 97.75% | 97.81% | 97.95% | 97.00% |
| M5 First / Last Trip Punctuality | 100.00% | 100.00% | 100.00% | 100.00% | 100.00% | 100.00% | 93.75% | 100.00% |

**Performance Statistics**
■ TARGETS HIT
■ TARGETS NOT ACHIEVED

**Above:** Keeping tabs on punctuality and the trams: In the NET Control Centre on 23 September 2019 this large display keeps staff up-to-date with current performance and tram availability. On tram availability it shows the booked number of trams in service (32), with one extra tram as a hot spare. Below this is the performance statistics for the previous week showing just the first/last trip punctuality measure had not been met on one day. The count on the right also indicates 197 days since the last accident.

**Above:** A view inside the control centre on 23 September 2019 showing the banks of screens which relay live images from CCTV of tram stops as well as the depot itself. *Robert Pritchard (2)*

locations of all trams on the network in real time, and also the status of all points and signals.

Controllers monitor power supply and radio contact is possible with tram drivers and other NET staff such as roving ticket inspectors on the network. They also have direct lines to Fire, Ambulance, Police, Traffic Control and Network Rail. Calls by passengers at help points go through to the control room to one of the duty network controllers. The control room staff have a myriad of information at their fingertips. For example the Citadis trams measure their capacity through the weight of the tram, so a particular tram can be brought up on the computer and staff can see what percentage of capacity it is operating at.

There are normally at least five people on duty in the control room. Adjacent to the control room is the customer services centre.

**Above:** Showing the scissors crossover just before the terminus, 224 heads away from the camera as it leaves Clifton South for Phoenix Park on 17 July 2016.

**Below:** A typical NET stop on segregated right of way – 217 arrives at Wilford Lane on 12 August 2021. Points of note include the stop signs, litter bin, shelter and information boards, ticket machine integrated with the PIS information screen which is attached to the top of the ticket machine, smartcard readers and the tall post incorporating the CCTV cameras. *Robert Pritchard (2)*

**Above:** Close up of one of the standard "next tram" indicators at stops, this one being at Cinderhill – the only platform served by trams travelling in opposite directions.

**Above:** Stops signs are often mounted with an integral litter bin underneath, as here at Rivergreen on the Clifton South line. Note the sign underneath that warns that the platform is a compulsory ticket area and warning of a £50 penalty fare or prosecution (this has since been increased to £70). *Robert Pritchard (2)*

Here 13 staff operate on a shift basis controlling both social media channels and any customer complaints and comments etc. They are in constant communication with the adjacent control centre, particularly at any times of disruption. Members of the customer services team can alert passengers instantly to any problems with services, using announcements, the passenger information displays or social media. These days social media is very different from when NET opened in 2004 and the company has a very active twitter account (@NETTram) and is also on Facebook.

## INFRASTRUCTURE

NET includes a number of significant infrastructure features such as bridges and viaducts as described in Chapter 3. Civil engineering work was particularly in evidence on the Phase 2 lines with eight new

bridges such as that at Nottingham station and a steel bowstring bridge at Queens Medical Centre crossing the city ring road. Major work was also undertaken on the Wilford toll bridge over the River Trent.

Like all urban tramways in the UK, NET is standard gauge (1435 mm). On the city centre street sections and on parts of the Phase 2 routes grooved tramway rail is used, mainly laid in continuous concrete slab with flush paving. To reduce noise rail joints were welded in situ. Most of the segregated sections of line use welded flat-bottomed rails of BS 80A profile on ballast with concrete sleepers, although there is some concrete slab track at certain locations. External contractors are used for rail grinding overnight as required.

To allow for flexibility during tram operations there are nine trailing crossovers across the system, which can also be used during times of emergency working or booked engineering blockades. There are also three scissors crossovers – at Station Street and the two Phase 2 termini at Toton Lane and Clifton South. Other points of note in terms of the track layout are the two centre turnback sidings at Clifton South and Beeston Centre stops and the bi-directional reversing siding at The Forest. There is an inbound loop line near University Boulevard stop and a recess siding at Wilford Lane.

In terms of the tram stops, there were 23 stops on Phase 1, including the three termini. This was more than doubled to 50 when Phase 2 opened. All have shelters built to a modular design and glazed with perch seating. Station Street, Queens Medical Centre and the two southern termini have rather more extensive covered waiting areas. Elevated cubes displaying the NET logo denote stops which also include Passenger Information Screens giving the destination and times the next trams are due, ticket machines, public address systems, travel information posters and timetables, rubbish bins, help points, smart card readers, passenger help points and CCTV cameras. There are also cycle storage facilities at some stops. The tram floor is 350 mm above rail level, giving virtually level access from stops. Ten stops have island platforms, these include the four stops on the northern stretch of the Hucknall route which is largely single track.

### THE POWER SYSTEM AND OVERHEAD LINES

Trams operating on NET use a single-arm pantograph to collect current from overhead power lines at 750 V DC, this power being fed through traction substations located around the system. The overhead line on the street sections uses span wires and on the off-street sections catenary suspension. The overhead wires are supported by a mix of overhead poles and direct fixings to adjacent buildings on the street running sections and especially in the city centre to minimise visual impact.

When the original line opened there were six electricity substations along the route each delivering 900 kW. The substations were initially located at Station Street, The Forest, Wilkinson Street depot, Highbury Vale, Moor Bridge and Butler's Hill and a further substation was later added at Basford. For Phase 2 seven further substations were built – on the Toton Lane line at Lenton Lane (alongside the bridge over the railway line), University Boulevard, Cator Lane and Inham Road and on the Clifton South line at Wilford Lane (part of the maintenance compound alongside the outbound platform), Clifton Centre and Clifton South. The substations are all painted in NET's distinctive dark green colours with a silver roof. They get their power from the National Grid via underground cables. It is possible for the control centre to isolate certain sections of the tramway so separate sections between any two substations can be taken out of service without affecting the rest of the network.

### SIGNALLING AND SIGNS

Most of the Nottingham Express Transit network uses "Line of Sight" signalling principles as used on other UK light rail systems with street running, allied to a Tram Management System supervisory system. This means that drivers should maintain a speed such that they can stop short of any obstructions simply by using the normal service brakes. Because of this the maximum speed on the on-street sections is generally the same as for motor vehicles on the stretch of

**Right:** Tram signal and signage at Moor Bridge, warning of the single line section ahead.

**Far right:** Tram signal and signage, including a 40 km/h speed limit sign, at the Phoenix Park terminus.

road in question (usually 30 mph in built-up areas). On segregated sections elsewhere the speed limit is generally up to 50 mph but is lower in some places for reasons of track alignment.

Some signalling is still needed at road junctions and crossings, ahead of single line sections on the Hucknall and Phoenix Park lines and on on-street sections to avoid conflicts with road traffic and because trams have a degree of priority over normal road traffic at some junctions.

To prevent confusion with conventional traffic signals, special white lights are used, and on the street-running sections these are often located above traffic lights. These signals consist of five white lights arranged either horizontally – telling a tram to stop, or vertically – telling a tram to proceed. A diagonal line pointing south-east to north-west indicates that a tram may proceed if turning left, and a diagonal line pointing south-west to north-east means that a tram may proceed if turning right. Five white lights arranged in the shape of a cross (known as a "cluster") in the centre of the indicator has the same meaning as an amber road signal: stop if it is safe to do so.

There are special arrangements on the single-track sections at the northern end of the system. Safe entry, still with the driver driving on line of sight, is indicated by the same signal aspects as at traffic controlled junctions but it is controlled by trackside equipment. Tram detection is by loops and points at the end of the single-track sections have sprung mechanisms to retain the point position for the normal facing point.

There are also points indicators on the approach to facing points and some trailing points to inform drivers which way the points are set and locked. As with the ordinary signals, these can show either a horizontal line for stop or a diagonal dogleg shaped line to indicate that the points are set for either a left or a right turn. All points within the depot are manual. General tramway signs such as speed limit signs are diamond shaped to avoid causing confusion to other road users.

**Below:** Tram stops are signposted with blue signs and the NET logo prominent.
*Robert Pritchard (3)*

**Above:** Various NET signage at the Clifton South terminus on 12 August 2021 as 225 awaits departure for Phoenix Park.

**Above:** There are special signalling arrangements on the single-track sections. On 30 December 2014 209 arrives at Moor Bridge with a service for Station Street. *Robert Pritchard (2)*

**CHAPTER 6:**

# SERVICES AND TICKETING

**Above:** Two Alstom Citadis trams pass at Nottingham Station on 30 June 2018, both operating on the longer of the two routes – 222 leaves heading towards the city centre and Hucknall as 219 approaches heading for Toton Lane. *Robert Pritchard*

Nottingham Express Transit operates two routes, one line is shown on the map in Green – from Hucknall to Toton Lane and one is shown in Purple – from Phoenix Park to Clifton South). The two routes can be summarised as follows:

- Hucknall–Toton Lane: 63 minute end-to-end journey time, 33 or 34 stops depending on direction;
- Phoenix Park–Clifton South: 46 minute end-to-end journey time, 27 or 28 stops depending on direction.

The two routes combine to give a very frequent service of either 12 or 16 trams per hour in each direction on the core section from Highbury Vale, through Wilkinson Street and the city centre to Nottingham Station.

The Monday–Friday service kicks off between 05.00 and 06.00 and then offers a 15-minute service on each route until 07.00, increasing quickly to every 7½ minutes until 10.00 when it reduces to a tram every 10 minutes until mid-afternoon, then increasing again to every 7½ minutes until around 19.00. It is then a 10 minute service again until 21.00 and then a 15 minute service until close of play. A significant difference on Saturdays is that the normal Monday–Friday peak service is kept in place right through the day – this means the service is more frequent during the middle of the day on Saturdays than on weekdays, but this caters for the many shoppers using the tram, people heading for trips out or to football matches and the like. The Sunday service is still very good, especially in comparison with some other tram systems, with a 10 minute service (the same as during the middle of the day on weekdays) in place for most of the day on Sundays. Standard frequencies are therefore as follows:

### Mondays–Fridays:

**Hucknall, Phoenix Park, Toton Lane/Clifton South to City Centre:**
- 06.00–07.00 and 21.00–00.00: Every 15 minutes
- 07.00–10.00 and 15.00–19.00: Every 7–8 minutes
- 10.00–15.00 and 19.00–21.00: Every 10 minutes

**Highbury Vale–City Centre (central section):**
- 06.00–07.00 and 21.00–00.00: Every 7–8 minutes
- 07.00–10.00 and 15.00–19.00: Every 3–4 minutes
- 10.00–15.00 and 19.00–21.00: Every 5 minutes

### Saturdays:

**Hucknall, Phoenix Park, Toton Lane/Clifton South to City Centre:**
- 06.00–07.00 and 21.00–00.00: Every 15 minutes
- 07.00–10.00 and 19.00–21.00: Every 10 minutes
- 10.00–19.00: Every 7–8 minutes

**Highbury Vale–City Centre (central section):**
- 06.00–07.00 and 21.00–00.00: Every 7–8 minutes
- 07.00–10.00 and 19.00–21.00: Every 5 minutes
- 10.00–19.00: Every 3–4 minutes

### Sundays:

**Hucknall, Phoenix Park, Toton Lane/Clifton South to City Centre:**
- 06.00–07.00 and 19.00–23.00: Every 15 minutes
- 07.00–19.00: Every 10 minutes

**Highbury Vale–City Centre (central section):**
- 06.00–07.00 and 19.00–23.00: Every 7–8 minutes
- 07.00–19.00: Every 5 minutes

Most trams cover the entire length of the route, but certain early morning and late evening journeys cover only part of the route as a way of getting trams to and from the depot. All trams start and finish the day at Wilkinson Street depot; the first departure from the depot is at 05.11 which then forms the 05.12 departure from Radford Road to Toton Lane. The last tram arrives back on the depot at night at 01.52, having worked the 01.05 from Toton Lane to Shipstone Street. This means that only between the hours of 02.00 and 05.00 are trams

Radford Road (05.12) to Toton Lane. Starting with the 06.01 departure from Toton Lane it then performs eight return trips from Toton Lane to Hucknall and back before doing the 00.50 from Toton Lane to Shipstone Street and then continuing empty to the depot at 01.37 – almost a 21 hour day in service!

There are short workings at times of day when the service frequency changes. Trams working down from Hucknall/Phoenix Park terminate at Wilkinson Street before working onto the depot and from Toton Lane/Clifton South terminate at Shipstone Street before going onto the depot. On the

not moving on or off the depot. Three early morning departures from the depot run empty stock to Nottingham Station from where they start their journey to Hucknall or Phoenix Park.

Despite these early services, NET's worst failing has always probably been the lack of services before 06.00, apart from the trams working from the depot to start the day meaning that provision for early shift workers who may need to travel before this time is poor. For example, the first departure from Toton Lane is 06.01, the first from Clifton South is at 06.02 and from both Hucknall and Phoenix Park at 06.04. All of these services reach the city centre around 06.25–06.30. The late night service is much better, however, with departures from the city centre until around 00.20–00.30 to all destinations and the very last departure from Old Market Square at 01.39 to Shipstone Street.

Trams are generally intensively diagrammed and most stay out in service all day, for example working timetable service number 1 is the first tram to depart the depot at 05.11 before starting in service from

**Above:** Citadis trams 230 and 235 pass at the Holy Trinity stop operating services on the Clifton South–Phoenix Park route on 13 February 2018. *Tony Christie*

Nottingham Trams Limited. Monday to Friday working timetable.

| | | | | | | | | | | | | | | | Non PMS | | Non PMS | | | Non PMS |
|---|---|---|---|---|---|---|---|---|---|---|---|---|---|---|---|---|---|---|---|---|
| **Service number** | 15 | 20 | 7 | 2 | 19 | 27 | 14 | 10 | 23 | 29 | 6 | 13 | 12 | 33 | 21 | 34 | 1 | 3 | 35 |
| Trip number | 1508 | 2011 | 709 | 212 | 1908 | 2711 | 1409 | 1012 | 2308 | 2911 | 610 | 1312 | 1210 | 3302 | 2109 | 3402 | 110 | 310 | 3502 |
| Replacement service | | | | | | | | | | | | | | | | | | | |
| Late | | | | | | | | | | | | | | | | | | | |
| **Hucknall** | 13:00:00 | | 13:10:00 | | 13:20:00 | | 13:30:00 | | 13:40:00 | | 13:50:00 | | 14:00:00 | | 14:10:00 | | 14:20:00 | 14:30:00 | |
| Butlers Hill | 13:02:00 | | 13:12:00 | | 13:22:00 | | 13:32:00 | | 13:42:00 | | 13:52:00 | | 14:02:00 | | 14:12:00 | | 14:22:00 | 14:32:00 | |
| Moor Bridge | 13:04:00 | | 13:14:00 | | 13:24:00 | | 13:34:00 | | 13:44:00 | | 13:54:00 | | 14:04:00 | | 14:14:00 | | 14:24:00 | 14:34:00 | |
| Bulwell Forest | 13:06:00 | | 13:16:00 | | 13:26:00 | | 13:36:00 | | 13:46:00 | | 13:56:00 | | 14:06:00 | | 14:16:00 | | 14:26:00 | 14:36:00 | |
| Bulwell | 13:08:00 | | 13:18:00 | | 13:28:00 | | 13:38:00 | | 13:48:00 | | 13:58:00 | | 14:08:00 | | 14:18:00 | | 14:28:00 | 14:38:00 | |
| **Phoenix Park** | | 13:42:00 | | 13:52:00 | | 14:02:00 | | 14:12:00 | | 14:22:00 | | 14:32:00 | | | | | | | |
| Highbury Vale Branch | | 13:44:50 | | 13:54:50 | | 14:04:50 | | 14:14:50 | | 14:24:50 | | 14:34:50 | | | | | | | |
| Highbury Vale | 13:09:50 | | 13:19:50 | | 13:29:50 | | 13:39:50 | | 13:49:50 | | 13:59:50 | | 14:09:50 | | 14:19:50 | | 14:29:50 | 14:39:50 | |
| Wilkinson Street | 13:15:00 | 13:50:00 | 13:25:00 | 14:00:00 | 13:35:00 | 14:10:00 | 13:45:00 | 14:20:00 | 13:55:00 | 14:30:00 | 14:05:00 | 14:40:00 | 14:15:00 | | 14:25:00 | | 14:35:00 | 14:45:00 | |
| **Depot** | | | | | | | | | | | | | | 14:24:00 | | 14:27:00 | | | 14:50:00 |
| The Forest | 13:21:00 | 13:56:00 | 13:31:00 | 14:06:00 | 13:41:00 | 14:16:00 | 13:51:00 | 14:26:00 | 14:01:00 | 14:36:00 | 14:11:00 | 14:46:00 | 14:21:00 | 14:29:00 | 14:31:00 | 14:32:00 | 14:41:00 | 14:51:00 | 14:55:00 |
| Royal Centre | 13:26:20 | 14:01:20 | 13:36:20 | 14:11:20 | 13:46:20 | 14:21:20 | 13:56:20 | 14:31:20 | 14:06:20 | 14:41:20 | 14:16:20 | 14:51:20 | 14:26:20 | 14:34:20 | 14:36:20 | 14:37:20 | 14:46:20 | 14:56:20 | 15:00:20 |
| Old Market Square | 13:28:20 | 14:03:20 | 13:38:20 | 14:13:20 | 13:48:20 | 14:23:20 | 13:58:20 | 14:33:20 | 14:08:20 | 14:43:20 | 14:18:20 | 14:53:20 | 14:28:20 | 14:36:20 | 14:38:20 | 14:39:20 | 14:48:20 | 14:58:20 | 15:02:20 |
| **Nottingham Station** | 13:32:00 | 14:07:00 | 13:42:00 | 14:17:00 | 13:52:00 | 14:27:00 | 14:02:00 | 14:37:00 | 14:12:00 | 14:47:00 | 14:22:00 | 14:57:00 | 14:32:00 | 14:40:00 | 14:42:00 | 14:43:00 | 14:52:00 | 15:02:00 | 15:06:00 |
| Queens Walk | | 14:09:00 | | 14:19:00 | | 14:29:00 | | 14:39:00 | | 14:49:00 | | 14:59:00 | | | | 14:45:00 | | | 15:08:00 |
| Wilford Lane | | 14:14:35 | | 14:24:35 | | 14:34:35 | | 14:44:35 | | 14:54:35 | | 15:04:35 | | | | 14:50:35 | | | 15:13:35 |
| Clifton Centre | | 14:22:55 | | 14:32:55 | | 14:42:55 | | 14:52:55 | | 15:02:55 | | 15:12:55 | | | | 14:58:55 | | | 15:21:55 |
| **Clifton South** | | 14:28:00 | | 14:38:00 | | 14:48:00 | | 14:58:00 | | 15:08:00 | | 15:18:00 | | | | 15:04:00 | | | 15:27:00 |
| NG2 | 13:36:35 | | 13:46:35 | | 13:56:35 | | 14:06:35 | | 14:16:35 | | 14:26:35 | | 14:36:35 | 14:44:35 | 14:46:35 | | 14:56:35 | 15:06:35 | |
| University of Nottingham | 13:43:20 | | 13:53:20 | | 14:03:20 | | 14:13:20 | | 14:23:20 | | 14:33:20 | | 14:43:20 | 14:51:20 | 14:53:20 | | 15:03:20 | 15:13:20 | |
| University Boulevard | 13:45:50 | | 13:55:50 | | 14:05:50 | | 14:15:50 | | 14:25:50 | | 14:35:50 | | 14:45:50 | 14:53:50 | 14:55:50 | | 15:05:50 | 15:15:50 | |
| Beeston Centre | 13:50:15 | | 14:00:15 | | 14:10:15 | | 14:20:15 | | 14:30:15 | | 14:40:15 | | 14:50:15 | 14:58:15 | 15:00:15 | | 15:10:15 | 15:20:15 | |
| Bramcote Lane | 13:58:00 | | 14:08:00 | | 14:18:00 | | 14:28:00 | | 14:38:00 | | 14:48:00 | | 14:58:00 | 15:06:00 | 15:08:00 | | 15:18:00 | 15:28:00 | |
| **Toton Lane 2** | 14:03:00 | | 14:13:00 | | 14:23:00 | | 14:33:00 | | 14:43:00 | | 14:53:00 | | 15:03:00 | 15:11:00 | 15:13:00 | | 15:23:00 | 15:33:00 | |

**Above:** An extract from the Nottingham Express Transit Monday–Friday Working Timetable (southbound services), showing three trams working off the depot and into service in the afternoon as part of the step-up of services mid-afternoon.

**Left:** Trams operate late into the evening on NET, although the early morning service has been criticised as starting up slightly too late. Night photography with modern digital cameras (or even smartphones!) can be rewarding in the city centre and produce pleasing results. On the evening of 4 September 2019 232 awaits departure from Old Market Square with an evening service for Clifton South.

where the first tram departs as early as 05.12 on all seven days of the week: not bad for a Sunday! The last southbound tram terminates at Nottingham Station, and the last three northbound trams likewise terminate at Shipstone Street. Thus, late night revellers are well catered for on NET, depending on where they live on the system.

## TRAM UTILISATION

Hucknall–Toton Lane route, the first two trams of the day northbound run only between Nottingham Station and Hucknall and the first five southbound trams run only between Radford Road and Toton Lane. At close of service, the last southbound tram from Hucknall terminates at Nottingham Station, and after the last northbound tram to cover the entire route leaves Toton Lane at 00.05 on Monday–Saturday nights and 23.05 Sunday nights there are then four more northbound workings that terminate at Shipstone Street, the last of which departs Toton Lane at 01.05 (00.05 Sunday nights) and arrives at Shipstone Street at 01.51 (00.51 Monday mornings).

Similarly, on the Phoenix Park–Clifton South route the first northbound tram of the day starts from Nottingham Station and the first four southbound trams start from Radford Road from

The initial NET timetable required 11 of the original fleet of 15 Incentro trams for service, operating a 10 minute timetable on each branch (Hucknall–Station Street and Phoenix Park–Station Street) at peak times, and a 12 minute service at off-peak times. An enhanced timetable from October 2005 saw this increased to 13 trams at peak times and 12 off-peak – a demanding target which continued until the Citadis trams entered service in summer 2014. An enhanced daytime frequency similar to that planned for introduction in 2015 was trialled in July 2014: this saw the now familiar frequency of a tram every 3–4 minutes on the core section at peak times and was possible thanks to the arrival of the Citadis trams. From 26 August 2014 the timetable had a tram running every 5 minutes on the core centre section.

**Above:** With a friendly wave from the driver, 217 accelerates along the straight section between Wilford Village and Wilford Lane – crossing one of the foot crossings on this section, with a service for Clifton South on 12 August 2021. *Robert Pritchard (2)*

**Above:** 226 has just left Southchurch Drive North heading for Phoenix Park on 17 July 2016. *Robert Pritchard*

**Above:** At the northern end of the network, 205 leaves Bulwell onto the single track section alongside the Robin Hood Line with a service for Hucknall on 19 June 2014. *Paul Abell*

**Above:** You can't miss the large NET ticket machines located at all stops! This double-sided one is located on the island platform at Wilford Village on the Clifton South line. At busier stops ticket machines are duplicated. *Robert Pritchard*

**Below:** A June 2014 poster illustrating how to operate the then new ticket machines that were being introduced on the network. *Paul Abell*

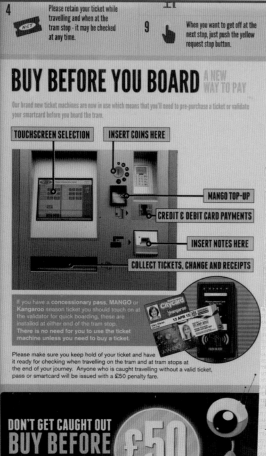

The opening of the new extensions in 2015 saw a rewrite of the timetable and this service pattern has been in place since then, albeit with some temporary changes during the Covid-19 pandemic (during times of crew shortages, including for most of January 2022, a Sunday timetable was in operation all week). The current working timetable calls for 32 of the fleet of 37 trams in service on Mondays–Fridays, 32 on Saturdays and 25 on Sundays. A further tram is designated a "hot spare" on the depot and available to come into traffic at short notice to replace any tram that may have to be withdrawn from service for whatever reason.

The working timetable shows that on weekdays off-peak, the Hucknall–Toton Lane service requires 15 trams, plus three additionals at peak times. The Phoenix Park–Clifton South route requires ten trams off-peak, plus an additional four at peak times.

The trams generally operate as a common user fleet – there had been a slight preference for diagramming the Incentro trams on the Phoenix Park–Clifton South route as this has slightly more off-street running than the Toton Lane route and the Incentros can take advantage of that as they have a slightly higher top speed, but the benefits to the timetable are negligible at a few seconds per trip.

### JUST THE TICKET

In the first ten years of operation, Nottingham Express Transit used conductors who issued and checked tickets on-board the trams. However, ahead of the Phase 2 extensions opening a decision was taken in May 2014 to abandon the policy of having conductors on trams in favour of ticket vending machines (TVMs) at all stops. This was the opposite of Birmingham's Midland Metro (now West Midlands Metro) and Sheffield Supertram, both of which originally used TVMs but later abolished them in favour of conductors as the TVMs were prone to vandalism (although at the time of writing it is understood that WMM is considering reverting to using TVMs). At the time, and with the system due to double in size, NET said it was simply not sustainable to keep conductors, and it was also difficult for them to get through and sell tickets on overcrowded trams. All current conductors were retrained as drivers and instead a system of roving ticket inspectors was employed. NET said its aim was that every passenger should have their ticket checked every six to seven journeys made, although the inspectors do tend to congregate around the city centre stops, hopping from tram to tram at frequent intervals.

Since this change of policy to a "Buy Before You Board" system, all passengers must buy a ticket from TVMs installed at all stops before boarding the tram unless they already hold a valid ticket, pass, smartcard or contactless payment card or device. Contactless payment was extended to NET in September 2021 and is also available on Nottingham City Transport buses and on the Linkbus network operated by CT4N but is only available for full price adult fares at present.

Initial adult single fares on NET when it opened in 2004 were between 80p and £1.20. A tram only day ticket was available for £2 or you could get a CityRider for use on the tram and Nottingham City Buses for £2.20. In 2022 an adult single for use between any two stops costs £2.50 if bought from a TVM or using the NETGO! app or contactless payment, or £2.40 if using a Robin Hood Pay As You Go smartcard. Smartcards and contactless bank cards and devices must be validated before boarding the tram by holding them over the validator on the TVM or the separate stand-alone validator provided at each stop. They do not also need to be held over a validator after alighting from the tram, however (doing so will result in you being charged for another journey if using Pay As You Go credit!).

A welcome innovation was the introduction of £1 short-hop cash singles available for journeys between any two stops within one of the nine short-hop zones which cover the whole system. These tickets offer excellent value for shorter single journeys, but they are currently only available as paper tickets from TVMs. The short-hop zones are:

- Hucknall Zone: Hucknall–Moor Bridge
- Bulwell Zone: Phoenix Park/Bulwell Forest–Basford
- Hyson Green Zone: Wilkinson Street–High School
- City Centre Zone: Nottingham Trent University–NG2/ Queens Walk
- QMC Zone: Gregory Street–University Boulevard
- Beeston Zone: Middle Street–High Road - Central College
- Bramcote Zone: Cator Lane–Toton Lane
- Wilford Zone: Meadows Embankment–Ruddington Lane
- Clifton Zone: Southchurch Drive–Clifton South

For children and young people under 19 a single journey costs £1.40 from a TVM or using NETGO! or £1.30 with a Robin Hood smartcard, and for students who hold a valid University of Nottingham or Nottingham Trent University ID card the single fare is £1.90 for a paper ticket or using NETGO! and £1.85 using a Robin Hood smartcard.

Day return tickets as such were withdrawn as part of a recast and simplification of NET fares in January 2019. However, a tram-only all-day ticket can be purchased for £4.40 adult, £3.40 student or £2.40 child bought from a TVM or using NETGO! Robin Hood smartcard holders who make at least two tram journeys in any one day receive an automatic daily price cap of £4.20 adult, £3.20 student or £2.30 child. For contactless card or device users the daily price cap is £4.40, the same as a paper all-day ticket. At present there is no daily price cap for passengers using more than one operator or mode of transport on the same day but this is expected to be introduced shortly.

Passengers travelling to sporting or cultural events at venues such as the Theatre Royal and Royal Concert Hall, Nottingham Playhouse, Nottingham Forest or Notts County Football Clubs can buy an Event Return from the TVM on the day of the event for £2.50. These must be shown with a valid event ticket if requested.

For anyone also wanting to travel on buses and/or trains a Robin Hood Day ticket is available for £5.40 adult or £3.20 child. These can be bought from TVMs at tram stops, on board the buses of participating operators (coins only and exact fare required on Nottingham City Transport buses if paying cash) and from train conductors if boarding at an unstaffed station. They can be used on the entire NET tram network and on all trains and almost all buses within the Greater Nottingham area. They are valid on trains between Nottingham and Bulwell, Carlton, Netherfield and Attenborough.

Robin Hood smartcard holders who also use their cards on buses receive a daily price cap of £5 adult, £4.30 student or £3.20 child. Robin Hood PAYG cards can be ordered online via the **www.robinhoodnetwork.co.uk** website or obtained from one of many Robin Hood Network TVMs located across Nottingham.

Alternatively, if travelling to Nottingham by train it is possible to buy a PlusBus ticket with your rail ticket giving unlimited travel on NET (except between Moor Bridge and Hucknall) and most buses within the Nottingham city boundaries for £5 on top of the rail fare (if staying at least one night in Nottingham, a PlusBus ticket can be purchased for either the day of arrival or the day of departure or both). This works out 40p cheaper than a Robin Hood Day Ticket but 60p more expensive than a tram-only all-day ticket so is only worth having if wishing to travel on both buses and trams. For railcard holders a Nottingham PlusBus ticket is £3.30 and thus worth buying even if only travelling on the trams. PlusBus tickets are automatically offered when buying train tickets online and can be requested when buying tickets from ticket offices and some TVMs.

At the time of this book going to press, pensioners and disabled people from within the Nottingham city boundaries or the rest of Nottinghamshire who hold concessionary travel passes issued by Nottingham City or Nottinghamshire County Councils may use their passes on NET between 09.30 and 23.00 on Mondays–Fridays and all day at weekends and bank holidays. Holders of concessionary passes issued elsewhere in the UK must pay the full fare if just making one single journey; however, holders of English National Concessionary Travel Scheme (ENCTS) passes issued by other English

local authorities who will be making at least two journeys on the same day can buy a special concession day ticket for £3 from the TVMs at tram stops. This ticket is known as a concession return but is an all-day ticket despite its name. Ironically, this means that before 09.30 and after 23.00 on weekdays, concessionary pass holders from outside Nottinghamshire can travel more cheaply than those who reside within the county who must pay for a full price adult ticket.

Seven day tram tickets are also available, from TVMs or via the NETGO! app for £19 for Adults, £14.50 for Students and £10 for Children. If paying in cash, due to limitations on the amount of change held in each ticket machine, £20 notes are only accepted for transactions over £10. Longer season tickets for one, three, six or 12 months are also available – the 12 month season is £550.

Any passengers who are found to be travelling without a valid ticket, pass or smartcard are subject to a Penalty Fare Notice. This was brought in during 2014 and was £50 initially, before being increased to £70 in October 2021. NET said that fare evasion during the pandemic rose to as high as 25% as Travel Officers were withdrawn. They were reintroduced in May 2021 and fare evasion then fell from 25% to 5%. Tramlink CEO Tim Hesketh said: "We are encouraged by the continued fall in fare evasion but 5% is still too high and that is why we are increasing the penalty fare as a further deterrent. Fare evaders are a small minority but their actions take the city and our loyal customers for a ride, undermining the huge efforts and investment we are all making to get Nottingham and the local economy moving again. With fares from just £1 it has never been easier to buy a ticket so our message to fare evaders is simple – do the right thing and pay your way to support your city."

## REQUEST STOPS

All stops on Nottingham Express Transit are officially request stops, meaning that passengers should press the stop request button to indicate that they wish to alight at the next stop. Unlike on buses and at railway station request stops it is not necessary to give a hand signal when boarding at an intermediate stop, however: just being clearly visible on the stop will usually suffice. In practice trams always stop at all the busier stops in the city centre anyway. For a time during the height of the Covid-19 pandemic from spring 2020 trams called at all stops by default and the drivers opened all doors so that passengers did not have to touch the door opening or the stop request buttons.

## RIDERSHIP FIGURES

Statistics from the Department for Transport show that the number of journeys on NET enjoyed steady but modest growth in the last few years before the Covid-19 pandemic but had fluctuated for the first few years of operation and dropped in the last few years before the Phase 2 routes opened. The target during the first full year was 8 million, which was surpassed. However, speaking at the official launch in 2004 Mike Casebourne from Arrow Light Rail Ltd predicted that NET Phase 1 could carry 11 million passengers in its first year, bringing in around £6.5 million of revenue and reducing car journeys in Nottingham by 2 million per year. In fact the 11 million figure was not reached until the Phase 2 extensions opened in 2015–16:

| 2003–04: | 0.4 million[1] |
|---|---|
| 2004–05: | 8.5 million |
| 2005–06: | 9.7 million |
| 2006–07: | 10.1 million |
| 2007–08: | 10.2 million |
| 2008–09: | 9.8 million |
| 2009–10: | 9 million |
| 2010–11: | 9.7 million |
| 2011–12: | 9 million |
| 2012–13: | 7.4 million |
| 2013–14: | 7.9 million |
| 2014–15: | 8.1 million |
| 2015–16: | 12.2 million |

| | |
|---|---|
| 2016–17: | 16.4 million |
| 2017–18: | 17.8 million |
| 2018–19: | 18.8 million |
| 2019–20: | 18.7 million[2] |
| 2020–21: | 3.4 million[2] |

[1] NET opened in March 2004 and thus only carried passengers for the last month of 2003–04.

[2] Ridership levels in 2020–21 were severely affected by the Covid-19 pandemic and travel restrictions put in place by the Government. Figures in 2019–20 were also affected by the start of the pandemic, and the national lockdown that was introduced on 23 March 2021 during the final weeks covered by these figures. During the pandemic Nottingham trams received grants totalling £18.5 million from the Department for Transport to maintain the tram service for key workers, the tram being particularly crucial for key workers as it serves the Queens Medical Centre.

A survey of usage patterns during the first year found that 34% of passengers were using the tram for commuting, 26% for shopping, 14% school and university trips, 11% visiting family and friends, 10% leisure and 2% for onward journeys such as rail or air. Before the tram 63% of these journeys were carried out by bus, 18% by car, 9% by cycle or on foot, 4% by train and 4% of journeys were not taken at all.

By the end of the second year growth had shown a 15.5% increase year-on-year. Overall, within the tram corridor, public transport trips were up 20% in the peaks compared with before the trams

**Right:** There are now smartcard validators installed at all tram stops. To use them, concessionary passes, Robin Hood smartcards or contactless bank cards should be touched on before customers travel on the tram. Passengers should make sure that they listen for the "beep" and see the green "tick" on the validator screen that confirms the touch-on has been recorded and the card is valid for travel. *Robert Pritchard*

**Above:** 233 arrives at Beeston Centre with a service from Toton Lane to Hucknall on 25 August 2015, the first day of service on the Phase 2 routes. Note the red window stickers announcing the opening. *Paul Abell*

railway station with the city centre and the north of the conurbation has profoundly affected life in the area with improved accessibility, reduced local congestion as well as acting as a catalyst for development and regeneration."

NET has consistently scored highly in subsequent passenger satisfaction surveys and won a number of awards at light rail events over the years. In an Institute of Customer Service (ICS) survey in 2019 NET scored 83 out of 100. The results showed NET had received an 8.5 out of ten rating when it comes to customers recommending the network to others. Customers also found Nottingham's trams easier to use than other forms of transport, rating the system 3 out of 10 for effort required (with 10 being the most difficult to use) compared to a transport sector average of 5. They also praised the competence and helpfulness of staff and their ability to explain information clearly.

arrived. According to a passenger satisfaction survey undertaken at this time, 80% of those interviewed wished to see NET extended to serve further routes. The overall service satisfaction after the second year was an impressive 94%. The Wilkinson Street Park & Ride also saw a remarkable increase in usage as passengers found that taking the tram into the city centre was preferable to driving there. Park & Ride by that stage accounted for 25% of tram passengers.

In a further boost to the system, in 2006 NET was voted the "best tram system in the UK" in a report by the Institute of Civil Engineers. The report said how well planned local transport systems can make a real difference to citizens' quality of life. The report said: "Nowhere is this truer than in Nottingham where the new tram system linking the

### USEFUL WEBSITES

- Nottingham Express Transit: *www.thetram.net*
- Robin Hood Network: *https://robinhoodnetwork.co.uk*
- Nottingham Contactless: *https://nottinghamcontactless.co.uk*

### ACCIDENTS

NET has a very good safety record, with only a relatively small number of accidents having occurred in its history. No trams have been involved in accidents bad enough to warrant major works attention. Some of the most notable incidents include:

- On 24 December 2004 a 32-year-old man suffered severe leg injuries after becoming trapped by a tram on Radford Road.
- On 6 October 2007 a 23-year-old man from Hucknall died after being hit by a tram when he stepped in front of it at Weekday Cross. This was the first fatality in the history of NET.
- On 11 November 2011 a 44-year-old man from Barnsley died after being hit by a tram near Wilkinson Street.
- On the evening of 28 November 2012 a 13-year-old girl was hit by a tram on the gated Bayles & Wylies foot crossing just north of Moor Bridge and later died from her injuries in hospital. This crossing, and the adjacent crossing over the Robin Hood Line, was later closed and replaced by a footbridge.
- In the late evening of 15 August 2016 a 51-year-old man was killed by a tram between David Lane and Basford after alighting at David Lane. He was spotted walking along the track, but misunderstandings between control staff meant that the tram driver was not warned of his presence. This led to a new procedure being introduced to deal with anyone observed in an off-street section of the tramway. This involves drivers stopping and control room supervisors monitoring CCTV at both ends of the section in which the person is reported. Normal working would only resume once two trams in both directions have confirmed the area is clear.

- On 25 May 2017 235 partially derailed at Old Market Square as it performed an out-of-course turn back move via the crossover just beyond the tram stop. It was rerailed later that evening.
- In the second serious incident in the city centre in just over a week, 229 was badly damaged (but not derailed) when it hit a delivery lorry on Victoria Street, near Old Market Square, on 3 June 2017.
- On 18 July 2017 a technical fault with the pantograph of a tram caused damage to the overhead wires near Basford, leading to severe disruption to services between David Lane and The Forest stops for the following three days.
- On 6 December 2017 a tram and a van collided on University Boulevard. Four passengers were slightly injured, and services were disrupted for a number of days afterwards.
- On 17 December 2017 the raincover of an empty pushchair became trapped in a tram door as the tram departed Radford Road stop. The Rail Accident Investigation Branch made a recommendation to all UK tram operators to carry out visual checks in addition to the automatic electronic door interlocking detection before a tram moves off.
- On 31 October 2018 226 was partially derailed after colliding with a car at Victoria Embankment, near the Meadows Embankment stop whilst working a Phoenix Park–Clifton South service. There were no major injuries, although the car driver received treatment at the scene. Services between Queens Walk and Wilford Lane on the Clifton line were suspended for more than three hours whilst the tram was rerailed.

**CHAPTER 7:**

# WHERE NEXT FOR NET?

In contrast to Manchester's Metrolink or London's Docklands Light Railway, which have expanded several times since the opening of their initial networks, to date NET's only expansion beyond its initial areas of operation have been the Phase 2 routes opened in 2015. A number of additions to the existing network have been mooted over the years; however, at the time of writing there are no immediate prospects of any further extensions. Indeed, in late 2021, it was reported that any extensions to the network had been delayed indefinitely because of coronavirus pandemic-related financial constraints – but they did remain a long-term aspiration.

In 2009, when Nottingham City and Nottinghamshire County Councils were seeking bids for the Phase 2 network, they put forward nine potential new tram routes, although at this point no detailed work had been done on any of these schemes:

- Hucknall–Linby.
- Phoenix Park–Kimberley and/or Watnall.
- Nottingham–West Bridgford, with a later extension to Gamston, Tollerton, Edwalton and Ruddington.
- Queen's Medical Centre–Arnold via Basford.
- Nottingham–Gamston.
- Nottingham–Gedling.
- Chilwell–Ilkeston.
- Chilwell–Stapleford and/or Sandiacre.
- Clifton to south-west of Clifton and towards East Midlands Airport.

Also considered at the same time was the possibility of tram-train routes to Gedling, Bingham and Ilkeston.

For several years from 2013, when the Phase 2 routes were being built, there were aspirations to extend the Toton line beyond its current southern terminus at Toton Lane to the now shelved HS2 East Midlands Hub at Toton (which was cancelled as part of the Department for Transport's Integrated Rail Plan for the North and Midlands published in November 2021). However, in early 2018 Nottingham City Council refused to pay for NET to serve the HS2 station, saying that funding for such an extension would have to come from the Government. However, HS2 high speed line promoter HS2 Ltd was also non-committal about a tram link to serve its station at Toton.

Meanwhile in 2011 the Kimberley, Eastwood & Nuthall Tram Action Group (KENTAG) was formed to campaign for an extension of NET to the satellite towns of Kimberley and Eastwood to the north-west of Nottingham. This scheme suffered a setback in December 2014 when Broxtowe Borough Council voted not to contribute £20 000 towards a £70 000 feasibility study for such an extension. In 2015 Broxtowe Council and the British Land Company jointly commissioned a £55 000 study by Mott Macdonald to examine options to reduce congestion along the A610 corridor through the borough. This considered four potential routes for a tram extension to Kimberley retail park.

In July 2018 Nottingham City Council approved funding for a £200 000 feasibility study for a number of potential new routes, with priority being given to an extension beyond the Clifton South terminus to the new 3000 home Fairham Pastures development next to the A453 road. The study was also expected to look at other potential new routes, including one serving the HS2 hub. In the autumn of 2019 Broxtowe Council commissioned a £100 000 survey from civil engineering consultants on an extension beyond the HS2 hub to Langley Mill and Kimberley. The council decided not to proceed with a survey of a further possible extension from Phoenix Park through Kimberley to the Ikea store at Giltbrook near Eastwood, however.

In March 2020 Nottingham City Council put forward proposals for extensions from Toton Lane via the HS2 station to Long Eaton, Derbyshire, from the Clifton South terminus to the Fairham Pastures development, and from near Nottingham station via Meadow Lane to Nottingham Racecourse Park & Ride to the east of the city centre with the potential to extend further to Gedling. It was hoped that construction of these three routes could start in 2025–26 for completion in 2028–29.

In May 2020 Light Rail Transit Association campaigning arm TramForward submitted even more radical proposals to the Government in a £2.7 billion plan known as the Midlands Connect Plan, which envisaged a further extension from the HS2 hub to Derby using tram-trains, which would form part of a new tram network for Derby using the old Great Northern Railway trackbed to Kingsway and serving the Royal Derby Hospital, Mickleover and Mackworth. The LRTA has also supported a tram-train route to East Midlands Airport, Loughborough and Leicester.

It remains to be seen if any of these schemes ever see the light of day, and one may well suspect that the shelving of the HS2 hub at Toton (along with the rest of the HS2 Eastern Leg to Leeds) will make this less likely for the foreseeable future.

## FURTHER READING ON NOTTINGHAM'S TRAMWAYS

- Lost Tramways of England: Nottingham, Peter Waller, Graffeg Ltd, 2018
- Nottingham's Growing Tramway: Building on NET's Success, Geoffrey Skelsey, LRTA, 2015
- Nottingham's Tramways, Philip Groves, Tramway Museum Society, 1978 (out of print)
- Nottinghamshire & Derbyshire Tramway, Barry M Marsden, Middleton Press, 2005
- Tramways of the East Midlands (LRTA Regional Handbook No. 1), R.J.S. Wiseman, LRTA, 2007

## ABBREVIATIONS USED IN THIS BOOK

- ABB: Allmänna Svenska Elektriska Aktiebolaget (ASEA) Brown Boveri
- AEC: Associated Equipment Company
- CCTV: Closed circuit television
- DC: Direct current
- ENCTS: English National Concessionary Travel Scheme
- EWS: English, Welsh & Scottish Railway
- GCML: Great Central Main Line
- GCR: Great Central Railway
- GRP: Glass Reinforced Plastic
- HS2: High Speed 2
- KENTAG: Kimberley, Eastwood & Nuthall Tram Action Group
- LED: Light-emitting diode
- LRTA: Light Rail Transit Association

- NCT: Nottingham City Transport
- NDE: Nottingham Development Enterprise
- NET: Nottingham Express Transit
- NHS: National Health Service
- OLE: Overhead line equipment
- P&R: Park & Ride
- PAYG: Pay As You Go
- PFI: Private Finance Initiative
- PTE: Passenger Transport Executive
- QMC: Queens Medical Centre
- STEM: Science Technology Engineering and Mathematics learning
- TVM: Ticket Vending Machine
- WMM: West Midlands Metro